D0857843

DOWN THE FAIRWAY

Published by
LONGSTREET PRESS, INC.
2140 Newmarket Parkway
Suite 122
Marietta, GA 30067

This book is reprinted in its entirety as it originally appeared in 1927, with the exception of the front and back matter, which have been updated.

Printed in the United States of America

2nd printing 2001

Library of Congress Catalog Card Number: 00-111983

ISBN: 1-56352-647-6

Jacket and book design by Burtch Bennett Hunter

DOWN THE FAIRWAY

The Golf Life and Play of Robert T. Jones, Jr.

By ROBERT T. JONES, Jr.
and O. B. KEELER

LONGSTREET PRESS
Atlanta

CONTENTS

FOREWORD to the 2001 Edition

By Jack Nicklaus

BOBBY Jones, my childhood hero, once wrote, "the stirring deeds of the great players of the past must always command the respectful attention of all who play golf at all regularly. To become reasonably knowledgeable in such matters comes close to being an obligation of the true golfer." Growing up in Columbus, Ohio, where Bobby Jones captured the 1926 U.S. Open Championship at the club of my youth, Scioto Country Club, I admired his contributions to golf from an early age. My father had followed the legendary Jones in 1926 and instilled in me an appreciation for the history of the game and the accomplishments of its greatest players, especially Bobby Jones.

The game of golf has enjoyed tremendous growth in recent years. The new millennium has already witnessed Tiger Woods win three consecutive major championships in the same year, sparking renewed excitement in golf and the inevitable comparisons of modern day champions to their predecessors. While the question of who was the better player makes for interesting discussion, it cannot and will not ever be answered. What we do know for sure is that every legend of our game made their own contributions and established their own records in their own times, inspiring future players to do the same in theirs. Any motivation the players of today might find in my past successes is due in no small part to the motivation I developed by studying the impressive record of Bobby Jones. In his time, Jones had no equal, capturing 13 major championships, four in the same year, and all of them in a span of just seven years. He retired from competitive golf at the age of 28 and went on to codesign Augusta National, which remains one of my favorite major championship venues. His impact on the game of golf, both on and off the course, has left a legacy that transcends time and will be talked about by golfers not yet born.

In 1927, at the age of 25, Bobby Jones—along with coauthor O. B. Keeler—penned *Down the Fairway.* That same year, the legendary Charles Blair Macdonald was recording his own reflections on the game in his autobiography *Scotland's Gift – Golf.* Macdonald, considered by many to be the father of American golf, attended the University of St. Andrews and brought his enthusiasm for golf back to his native Chicago at a time when the game was still in its infancy in the United States. In his book, written almost three-quarters of a century ago, Macdonald addressed this difficulty that remains with us today and will, no doubt, be with us as long as the game is played—determining who is the greatest player of all time.

> "While I'm writing the above, July 15, 1927, a cablegram is shown me from St. Andrews that Bobby Jones has won the open championship with a record score of 285 at St. Andrews. I have always thought young Tom Morris was the greatest golfer that ever lived; today I believe that Bobby Jones is equally wonderful. He is, as it were, the reincarnation of young Tom. I have known both more or less intimately and I am familiar with the conditions under which both played, conditions today and those from the early 1870s; young Tom on an unkept, rough course with the gutta ball, Bobby on

a smooth, park-like, perfectly kept course with a rubber-cored ball. To my mind, these two are the greatest golfers in history, both as to execution, clean sportsmanship, courtesy, equable temperament, and most attractive personality."

Macdonald's words seem as appropriate today as they did in 1927. For me, all any player can do is compete to the best of his ability in his own era. Bobby Jones, as much as any player in history, was the greatest player of his time. While comparisons between players of different generations will always be made, I believe it is more important that we always maintain a sense of history and a healthy respect for the accomplishments of those who've come before us. Ultimately, Jones' records—like mine and those being amassed by today's champions—become part of the lore and legacy of golf to be debated and interpreted for generations to come.

Down the Fairway is one of the finest books ever written on golf and a must-read for anyone who loves the game. For some, the rerelease of this book will serve as an introduction to Bobby Jones. In that case, it is a wonderful tool to connect the past and the present as new readers develop their own appreciation for one of golf's greatest players. For others, this book will be an opportunity to revisit a piece of the rich history that makes the game of golf so special. For all of us, it is a chance to enjoy a truly timeless story from one of the game's legends.

JACK NICKLAUS
February 2001

FOREWORD

By Grantland Rice

ABOUT one person in every ten million might have an interesting autobiography to put out at the age of twenty-five. Bobby Jones in this respect is one among ten millions. This is supposed to be the age of youth in sport, but Bobby was the super-youth; for he was almost a seasoned competitor, a competitor meeting and beating champions, at the age of fourteen. The entire history of sport has never recorded another such incident. At the age of twenty-five Bobby Jones had had thirteen years of campaigning. At that same age he had won almost every championship known to golf, through a vivid personal experience few competitors ever get to know at the age of sixty.

Bobby Jones has been something more than one of the most skilled shot makers in the span of golf. Back of this amazing skill there have also been character, magnetism, courage, and intelligence of a high order. He has been the ideal sportsman in every contest, always scrupulous in observing not only the letter of the rules but the spirit of the game. He set certain high ideals from the start of his career and he has never wavered from the line in the slightest way since the start. One of the finest tributes ever paid Jones came from an opponent, who once made this remark: "The chief weakness with Bobby is that he goes out of his way too much to encourage and cheer up his opponents when things are not breaking too well."

His golf record is remarkable. At the age of twenty-five he

had won the United States Open twice, from the best professionals and the best amateurs. He had won the British Open. He had won the Amateur Championship of the United States twice. For a period of five years he had never finished lower than second place in United States Open Championships, facing the best golfers in the game. There have been many in golf who were brilliant on their big days. But consistency and brilliancy have rarely mixed in this most uncertain of all games. It remained for Bobby Jones to find the mixture which so many others have sought for so long a time. The start of Bobby Jones' career to date is one of the most interesting episodes in all sport, one of the most unusual of all careers. Although Bobby Jones can write extremely well, he was fortunate in having the co-operation of O. B. Keeler, an able golf historian who has followed almost every stroke of his career.

The story of Bobby Jones is truth that is stranger and far more interesting than fiction, a saga of youth that could only be sung in the modern game.

GRANTLAND RICE
June 21, 1927

DOWN THE FAIRWAY

PART ONE

CHAPTER ONE

BEGINNINGS

SOME way, autobiography and memoir always have been words associated in my mind with persons who were dead, or at least very old. And certainly I am not yet sufficiently reconciled to the idea lately suggested, that I write a memoir, to go about it in any familiar way. I continue to feel that I ought to be old, if not actually dead. And I'm not so old—twenty-five on St. Patrick's Day, 1927. Still, as Georgie Low said, golf is an 'umbling game. And I can add earnestly that it is an aging game. Tournament golf, I mean. You may take it from me that there are two kinds of golf; there is golf—and tournament golf. And they are not at all the same. It took me a good many years to find that out, and perhaps it cost me a few tournaments. . . . I've been in quite a number, you see.

Twenty-one national championships, counting only the biggest ones; and more than a hundred smaller tournaments and exhibition matches and lesser competitions. Twenty-one national championships in ten years seem a lot of championships, considered all at once. Especially when you've won only five of them. But the ten years seem to have been very long years, looking back across them to the Merion Cricket Club near Philadelphia—odd name for one of the finest of golf courses—where, in 1916, as a kid of fourteen I was in my first national tournament, scared stiff at the end of the first qualifying round when I found myself leading the field. I struck a proper average by leading the field at the other end, in the afternoon round. . . . Ten years ago—but I suppose memoirs should extend farther back than that. So I will go back as far as I can remember, when I was just about as unpromising a prospect for a golfer, not to say a champion, as you can well imagine.

Judging from certain photographs I must have been an odd-looking youngster. I started out with an oversize head and a spindling body and legs with staring knees, and some serious digestive derangement which caused my parents and six or seven doctors a deal of distress. Dad says I didn't eat any real food until I was five years old, but I don't remember about that. I must have been pretty frail because I don't remember any playmates while we lived on Willow Street in Atlanta, except Camilla, our fat cook and nurse, and her fat brother, who was also blacker than Camilla; and Camilla's beau. I used to enjoy the visits of Camilla's brother, who sat on the back veranda while I rode my velocipede there, and taught me to swear and call Camilla's beau all kinds of curious names. Occasionally Camilla took me to her home for a little visit and I have a distinct recollection of falling off the rear veranda of her house head first into a garbage can. It is lucky for me that I do not have to trust everything to memory, for I have no independent recollection of ever getting out of the can. I had a big black and white collie named Judge, who caused me a lot of trouble by following people away from our house; he would follow anybody, and I had to go and bring him back. I liked the ice-man too—that was Camilla's beau—and when he came to deliver the ice I liked to get out on the street and hold my hands under the block as he sawed it, and catch the ice sawdust (I thought it was that) and eat it. The only memory of other children at this time is a vague recollection of a party where we tried to pin tails on a donkey's picture and I won a prize by pinning a tail just under his nose—an award which puzzles me to this day.

When I was five years old we went to live at the Corinthian Apartments in West Peachtree Street and I must have perked up a bit, as I was playing baseball most of the time on a vacant lot across the street. I must have been deeply interested in baseball because I remember with a peculiar vividness an organ-grinder who came around with a monkey, and the accuracy with which the monkey could catch a ball. I envied that monkey. Indeed, I had a hazy wish to be a monkey and astonish the boys by my skill at catching the ball. In those days I used to catch behind the bat without a mask—our appliances were limited—and was rather proud of the position, which was regarded as dangerous. One day Bob Ravenel swung too hard at a pitched ball, the bat came all the way round, slipped out of his hands, and cracked me on the side of the head. I ceased to be a hero at once; I never went behind the plate again.

It was about this time I started to school, the Woodbury School, populated mostly by girls—very large girls, it seemed to me. There were only three or four boys in my department, and they were very small boys and inconspicuous. I always had a sort of oppressed feeling at that school, besides which I had whooping cough, measles, and other juvenile ailments in rapid succession, and couldn't attend regularly, and one day Dad asked me if I would rather keep on going to school or stop and play ball. As a choice this was the easiest I can remember.

Up to this time I never had heard of golf. There was no golf tradition in our family. Dad had been a crack ball-player at college, but he had never taken up golf. He was not encouraged parentally to play baseball. My grandfather, Robert Tyre Jones, for whom I was named, was—and is—an old-fashioned, sturdy business man of Canton, Georgia, who set his foot down solidly when he learned that Dad, on being graduated from the University of Georgia, had signed a contract to play with the Brooklyn Club of the old National League. Dad's budding career as a big-league ball player was nipped right there. He told me once that Grandfather never would go to see him play ball. That was when Grandfather came down to Atlanta to watch me play in a Red Cross golf match in 1918, with Perry Adair against Jimmy Standish and Kenneth Edwards. Dad said I ought to feel highly honored, because Grandfather never had shown the slightest interest in sports before. And he never did admit he had come down to watch me play golf! And when the Atlanta party went to New York to meet me last July, coming home from England after winning the British open championship, of course Mary—that's Mrs. Jones—was there, and Dad and Mother and Grandmother, too. And there was Grandfather! He told the newspapermen he happened to be in New York on business! I never will forget the first telegram he sent me, when I was away playing in a championship. It was at Inwood in the American open of 1923. "Keep the ball in the fairway," it said, "and make all the putts go down." I can tell you, I found my eyes stinging, when I read that. . . . It was at Inwood I finally managed to break through, winning in a playoff after a tie with Bobby Cruickshank.

Golf began for all of us—Mother and Dad and me—in the early summer of 1907, when we moved out of the city to board with Mrs. Frank Meador in a big house about a mashie pitch from what was then the second fairway of the East Lake golf course of the Atlanta Athletic Club, five miles from town. There was plenty of interest out there in the country—a big stable, a garden full of raspberries and a fair supply of snakes to kill, and a creek which could be dammed for hypothetical fishing purposes; we never caught any fish but never got over the idea that we would catch them.

Frank Meador, two years older than I, lived there, and several young men, boarders, who played golf at East Lake. It was one of these, Fulton Colville, who gave me my first club, a cleek which he had discarded and cut down to my size. Frank was already making hesitating efforts at playing this queer new game, and as they wouldn't allow kids to go on the course, we made a course of our own. It consisted of two holes, exactly the same in length, as we played one and then played back to the other. One hole was in the roadway in front of the house, which extended into the main road alongside the East Lake club property. The other hole was the deep ditch on the farther side of the main road, a hundred yards away; any part of the ditch. Sometimes when the fairway, or roadway, was dry and hard we could hit a ball that would go rolling into the ditch from what constituted the tee. It is a matter of rather general opinion that I never made a hole in one shot until

1927. I made this hole several times in one shot, before I was six years old. True, it was not the orthodox hole of four and a quarter inches; most golfers would regard it a hazard rather than a hole. But it suited Frank and me well enough and kept our medal scores down.

I wish I could say here that a strange thrill shot through my skinny little bosom when I swung at a golf ball for the first time; but it wouldn't be truthful. I do not remember the first time I hit a golf ball, or hit at one; and as I recall it the game did not make much of an impression on me, except that I used to get mad enough to dance in the road when a wild shot went under a little bridge covered with briers across the ditch which was not the second hole. I liked baseball much better, and played golf, or what we called golf, because of a dearth of boys in the neighborhood with whom to play baseball. Mother and Dad had taken up the game and played regularly at the East Lake course. Jimmy Maiden was the professional there at the time and he gave them lessons. Nobody paid much attention to Frank and me and I am sure neither of us entertained any profounder ideas about the game than that golf balls were easy to lose and hard to come by. When Mother and Dad moved back to the city in the fall of 1907, I went back to baseball at once and that winter learned to drive my first automobile—a Glasscock Racer, it was called, operated by pumping a lever. It had brakes and I loved to pump it at top speed straight for a corner and then, with Mother or Camilla shrieking at me, jam on the brakes and pull up unconcernedly in a couple of yards.

We moved back to East Lake the next summer, in 1908, and here I ought to be able to record another sensation, because soon afterward Stewart Maiden came to be professional at the club, and that was the very luckiest thing that ever happened to me in golf, which is saying a lot, because my entire career, if it may be called a career, has been lucky. There were times, during what one writer called my seven lean years, when I fancied most of the luck was bad luck; but I was wrong. Some people can learn only by having education drubbed into them; and I want to say right now that I never learned anything from a match that I won. Not until the seven lean years were over, at any rate. . . . But the best luck that ever I had in golf was when Stewart Maiden came from Carnoustie, Scotland, to be professional at the East Lake club. So I'd like to record a sensation, when I went with Mother to meet Dad at the suburban car one evening just at dusk, and we went over to the gate of the club, and joined Jimmy Maiden—Stewart's brother, who preceded him—and Stewart, who had just arrived.

But there was nothing sensational about Stewart. He said very little and I couldn't understand a single word of what he said; he was not long over from Scotland. Jimmy and Dad and Mother did the talking, and at first I wondered if Stewart could talk at all. Jimmy was going away and Stewart was taking his place. Carnoustie has furnished the East Lake club with five professionals—Alex Smith, Jimmy Maiden, Stewart Maiden, Willie Ogg, and Charlie Gray, who recently was Stewart's assistant there.

No—there wasn't any sensation, any more than when I swung the first time at a golf ball. Stewart was just another little Scot, like Jimmy, only Scotcher. But it wasn't long before I was following him about the East Lake course and watching him. Mother and Dad were playing a lot now and they let me go around with them occasionally, on condition that I would take only one club and keep up with them, which was out of the question if I carried my entire outfit, which by this time consisted of a brassie of Mother's, cut down; a mashie discarded by Dad; and the faithful cleek, which I used as a putter, and, indeed, for most other shots. I kept up pretty well by simply beating the ball along, rarely getting the chance to hole out. When I followed Stewart, I didn't carry even one club. I just watched him. I never was conscious of studying his play, or of trying to play like him. I liked golf pretty well; he was the best player at the club; and I liked watching him perform. He paid little or no attention to me, and after tagging along four or five holes I would leave the match and go back to our house—we had moved into a cottage inside the club property, right by the thirteenth green of the old course—and get a cap full of old balls and my mashie and putter and go out to the thirteenth green and pitch them all on and putt them all out, over and over again. It was pretty good practice, I suppose. I liked to pitch the ball, and as I recall it I could get it close to the pin with a fair consistency. . . . Lately I have caught myself thinking about those long, sunny afternoons, pitching balls at the pin on the old thirteenth green, and I've wished I could get the ball up there as accurately now, from proportionate distances. The short pitch is the weakest spot in my game, these last few years. Maybe I've got away from Stewart Maiden's method that was so clearly before me in those days when I had so little else to think about.

I don't know about that, either. I don't remember any glimmering thought of form, in golf, or any consciousness of a method in playing a shot. I seemed merely to hit the ball, which possibly is the best way of playing golf; certainly it is the easiest on the mind. Besides, I was interested in other things—tennis and fishing, mainly, now that I had access to a regular lake and the club's tennis courts. Golf still was incidental; I played at it as I played at anything else that came along and seemed attractive; if I have any genius at all, it must be a genius for play! I love to play—I love fishing and hunting and trapshooting and ping-pong and chess and pool and billiards and driving a motor car, and at times I love golf, when I can get the shots going somewhere near right. It seems I love almost any pursuit except work. I even like going to school, which I am doing again, right now. But I didn't like going to school, at the time of which I am writing. I even evolved a wicked habit of walking in mud-puddles on the way to school to get my feet impossibly wet so I would be sent home, when I would go fishing or to play golf or tennis. But not often—only when I felt I could not stand that particular day in school. . . . It was one of these excursions that got me my only whipping from Dad. I had been sent home from school and Dad happened to be late going to town and he suspected my ruse and forbade me expressly to go fishing that day, or to go near the lake. As soon as he departed I went down to the boat-house and began fishing from the little dock. I hooked a fish and yanked it up in the air. It was the biggest fish I ever had caught, and in my excitement, instead of swinging the fluttering prey inward to where I could grasp it, I stepped right off into water about six feet deep. I couldn't swim a stroke and these memoirs probably are due to the fact that Ed, the boat-house attendant, was near and hauled me out. That gained me my first and last licking from Dad.

Now, I suppose that all the time I was watching Stewart play golf the imitative faculty which seems inherent in most children was at work, and that I began hitting the ball as he did, so far as my limitations would permit. Dad says I was a natural mimic in those days, and I remember he used to amuse a veranda full of people at times by inspiring me to get out on the lawn and imitate the swing of this player or that one—usually someone in the gathering. There was one of our good friends, Judge Broyles, who never seemed to get as much fun as the others out of my imitation of his own style. He used to carry his own clubs, and, when preparing to play a shot, he laid the bag down carefully by his left foot, took his stance, addressed the ball, swung, and with his eyes following the flight of the ball released the grip of his left hand from the club, stooped, grasped the bag of clubs, and set out at once at a slow trot after the shot. . . . I could go out and show you Judge Broyles' "follow-through"—as they called it—right now. He was a whimsical character. At our house we always had a midday dinner on Sunday, as there invariably was a lot of golf played and the players spent the day—the late George Adair, Tick Tichenor, Dowdell Brown, and others. Perry Adair, the first boy wonder of Dixie, and Frank Meador and I always played golf, too, and we had a small table to ourselves at dinner, and I remember how I used to wonder at Judge Broyles' custom of bringing with him a supply of goose-liver sausage and rye bread, which he would eat for his dinner instead of the fried chicken, rice and gravy and hot biscuits prepared by the faithful Camilla as the conventional southern repast for Sunday dinner.

It was at one of these dinners I caused more than a ripple by inquiring from our small table during a lull in the conversation:

"Dad, what do people do on Sunday who don't play golf?"

Yet when I was eight and nine years old I was playing more tennis than golf and at ten Frank and I got into a regular competition—the club championship. We had been playing together a lot and somebody suggested as a joke that we enter the tournament. We took the suggestion seriously, our entry was accepted and we were duly paired for the first round with Carleton Smith and Eston Mansfield, one of the greatest teams southern tennis ever produced. The ensuing match must have been edifying; certainly the little knot of gallery on the small green grandstand—we were playing on No. 1 court—was appreciative enough.

Carleton Smith had an odd serve; a sort of half-Lawford, which bounded high and crankily, and if I stood in the usual position to receive, at the base-line, the ball invariably bounded so high over my head I couldn't reach it. So I received Carleton's service with my back against the wire netting of the backstop, at a distance where it required a hard swing to get the ball back over the net. My own serve was modeled—as I fondly believed—on that of Ed Carter, a tall, powerful player with a full-arm, slashing "American" service. When I confronted Carleton and began tossing the ball well up in the air and unwinding my idea of the "American serve," I could hear shouts of encouragement from the gallery.

"Hit it hard, Bob—knock him down!"

I hit the ball as hard as I could, and Frank and I worked like mad, and Carleton and Eston and the gallery had a wonderful time, while it lasted. Our tenure in the tournament was fervid, if brief. And that is about my farthest north, in tennis.

Remembering childhood is rather confusing; so many things happened, and their chronology is sort of flat, as if everything had happened pretty much all at once, as things do in dreams. I have got away up to where I played in the Atlanta Athletic Club tennis championship, and here I am recalling an elderly pony I used to ride a lot when I was living over in the Meador house outside the East Lake Club property, which was at least four years earlier. I guess that pony must have been thirty or forty years old, and she was set in her ways, one of which was to start off always in the wrong direction as she trotted out of the gate. She would turn to the right every time, and our hired man, Wiley, became so accustomed to this idiosyncrasy that as soon as I had scrambled onto the pony's back he would go to the gate and get ready to catch her and turn her back toward the club. I loved that old pony and named her Clara, after my mother—a compliment which Mother seemed not to appreciate properly.

The first competitive golf I played was at the age of six years, when I won my first cup. . . . I have it today, and I'll keep it always; a tiny cup three inches tall, and a cup that I'll always feel I am not entitled to keep.

There was a party at Mrs. Meador's when our family was living there. Alexa Stirling, who later won the women's national championship three times in succession, lived in the neighborhood, and Frank Meador of course lived at the same house I did, and Perry Adair was invited and Mrs. Meador arranged a medal competition; six holes on the old East Lake course, and provided this little cup as the trophy. . . . If Mr. Maeterlinck is right, and if the past, present and future really are co-existent, I'd love to go over that round of six holes again and check it up. Because I'll always believe Alexa won that cup. Frank Meador, however, figured it out that I won it, and as his mother was giving the cup, we regarded Frank as having something like a plenary connection with it, so it was awarded to me. . . . I took it to bed with me that night. . . . I've a hundred and twenty cups and vases now, and thirty medals, but there's one little cup that never fails of being kept well polished. And I never slept with another one.

Then a little later Mrs. E. G. Ballenger promoted another tournament, a match-play affair this time, and we were handicapped according to age; so Perry had to give me one stroke a round, and we met in the finals, which were 36 holes—the same distance as the finals of a national championship today. We played our match on Sunday, and I remember how important I felt, with the fourball matches all over the East Lake course giving way to Perry and me—standing aside politely while we went through, because we were playing a tournament match! I'll say this for us, we didn't hold anybody up. Our method in golf was simple and rapid. We walked up to the ball and socked it. We didn't sock it far. I suppose we could drive slightly over a hundred yards, but we rarely got off the line. And on the green we didn't squat down and line up our putts. We walked up to the ball and knocked it at the hole. And (if memory is at all reliable) it is amazing now, the proportion of putts that went into the hole.

Now and then, when I'm playing behind some slow match, and watching the members lining up a three-footer from both ends, and picking up gravel along the supposed path of the putt, I think of George Duncan's suggestion as to putting:

"The best system," says George, "is to go up to the ball and knock it into the hole!"

And Alex Smith, who was always a good putter, never fooled around over a putt.

"Miss 'em quick!" was Alex's motto. And he didn't miss so many, at that. Also, he never bothered about picking up little impediments along the path of the putt.

"Won't those things throw the ball off the line?" he was asked.

"Just as likely to throw it on the line!" rejoined Alex.

I never have believed in hanging over a shot, and until the last two years I was as prompt on the putting green as with any other shot. They say now that I am studying my putts more carefully. That is not all of the truth. I do study them a bit more; until I can see the "line," I won't putt, now. In the old days I didn't like the idea of slowing up the round, and if I couldn't see the line, I'd putt anyway. . . . Seeing the line is a curious thing and I am free to confess I do not well understand it. I suppose it's one of the psychological phases of golf. In some rounds, when I am scoring well, the line of every putt is as plain to me as if someone had drawn it in whitewash, and I can see just how much to "borrow" from a slope, and exactly where the door to the cup is. Other days the line is dim and I have to look for it carefully.

But most of the time I take on the green today is not looking for the line or cleaning off the path of the putt. At Merion, in 1924, when I first won the United States amateur championship, eight years after I started in that fixture on the same course, I found that I was walking rapidly up to a green and putting promptly, while my breathing still was hurried and irregular. . . . I always walk fast between shots, and up to the last two years they have said that George Duncan and I were the fastest players in the world. Today I don't take a great deal of time, I think. But at Merion I resolved never to make a putt in an important round while my breathing was hurried. So I'd look over the line of the putt, and maybe even sit down to consider it, apparently. But my object was to get my breathing and heart tranquillized. It's a small thing. But championship golf is perhaps the closest business in the world, and it's the small things, down to the single blade of grass which turns your ball off from the cup, that make up the margin between first-class players. They said I putted well at Merion. One of the dearest compliments I've ever had paid me was when Grantland Rice told me that Jerry Travers, that master-putter, had watched me in the final match and said he never had seen a more beautiful putting stroke. Maybe the tranquillized breathing helped. Anyway, it didn't hurt.

Perry and I didn't bother about our breathing or tranquillizing our heart action in that 36-hole match; we continued to walk up to the ball for every shot and sock it, and I suppose we got around that course in about two hours—no more—and we went around it twice and I won, 2-1, at the thirty-fifth green. It was a tiny vase I got, this time.

What a wonderful thing it is now, to think of that time when golf meant only to go up to a ball and sock it; when golf was only a game, and a match was only a match, with dear little Perry to beat if I could—not all cluttered up with silly notions of championship! One of these days I'll hang up the old clubs, so far as championship golf is concerned, and I'll be happier then. But it never can be again what it was when Alexa and Perry and I first played. The glare of championship takes the dew quickly off the turf!

CHAPTER TWO

I DISCOVER OLD MAN PAR

THE first big cup I won—comparatively big—was the junior championship cup of the Atlanta Athletic Club. I was nine years old, and it was a formal tournament. Howard Thorne, who was a big boy, sixteen years old, beat Perry Adair in the semi-final round and I beat Howard, 5-4, in thirty-six holes. My picture was printed in The American Golfer at the time. . . . The same magazine printed the same picture last year, after the United States open championship; a scrubby, towsled-haired kid with skinny arms and legs and a finish indicating a flatter swing than I have now. With it was printed a picture of Jess Sweetser as a youngster. "They hold all the major championships there are," said the caption. . . . But I was prouder, that first time the funny little picture was published.

Next year, in 1912, Howard beat me in the semifinals of the same championship, and Perry beat him in the finals. Perry was beginning to step out, and a year or two later he was the Boy Wonder of Dixie in the headlines, and went to the finals of the southern amateur championship, defeating his father, George Adair, on the way and losing to Nelson Whitney in the last round. I was shooting down around 90 and occasionally a stroke or two below at the time of the club championship in 1912, and the old course at East Lake was a tough scoring proposition. The original course was an odd affair, as I recall it. The first hole was a pitch of 165 yards; the third was another pitch or medium iron shot, and those were the only par 3 holes on the course. After passing the third hole, there was a gruelling stretch of fifteen holes without a short one, and most of them were long two-shotters, the hardest type of hole on which to keep scoring par. This course was greatly altered in 1914 when George Adair and Stewart Maiden came back from a tour of Great Britain—Mr. Adair took Perry along, I remember—and the present course is nothing like the old one, though a few of the original holes still are in play. Stewart says the present course, while longer, is easier to score on.

It was in 1913, the year before the old course was changed, when I was 11 years old, that two things happened to me that now seem worthy of note, as influencing my association with golf. Up to that time, as suggested, golf was rather an incidental matter along with tennis and fishing and baseball; it was just another game, and if I could beat somebody at it I felt I had achieved something, just as when I managed to defeat someone at tennis, or when our side won at baseball. I suppose I never had the least notion that golf offered more than merely personal competition, as a game. Even when we had a medal round, I was trying to beat Perry or whoever seemed the most dangerous competitor. I kept my scores in every round of golf as a matter of course; and naturally I liked to get under 90. But the scoring, of itself, was relatively a detached part of the affair, which, to my way of thinking, was a contest with somebody—not with something.

It may not be out of place here to say that I never won a major championship until I learned to play golf against something, and not somebody. And that something was par. . . . It took me many years to learn that, and a deal of heartache.

It was in 1913 that Harry Vardon and Ted Ray came over from Britain to play in our national open championship at Brookline, and Francis Ouimet, then a boy of 19, shot his way into a triple-tie with the famous English professionals and beat them in the playoff. That is the first golf I remember reading about in the papers, and I began to feel that this was a real game. In October, Vardon and Ray played an exhibition match at East Lake with Stewart Maiden and the late Willie Mann, then professional at the new Druid Hills Golf Club in Atlanta, and defeated our boys 1 up, Ray having to sink an eight-foot putt on the thirty-sixth green to get a half and win the match.

This was the first big match I had ever watched and I followed every step of the 36 holes. Ray's tremendous driving impressed me more than Vardon's beautiful, smooth style, though I couldn't get away from the fact that Harry was scoring more consistently. Par—par—par, and then another par, Harry's card was progressing. They played 36 holes at East Lake and 36 more at Brookhaven next day, and I remember Vardon's scores: 72-72-73-71; a total of 288, or an exact average of 4's all the way. I remember thinking at this time, and it would be difficult to find a better illustration, that 4's seemed to be good enough to win almost anything. Today I would not qualify the estimate. I'll take 4's anywhere, at any time.

On the twelfth hole of the afternoon round at East Lake, Ted Ray made a shot which stands out in my mind today as the greatest I have seen.

Our boys had finished the morning round 2 down but had started brilliantly after luncheon, especially Stewart, and had got in the lead. Then, beginning with the twelfth hole, the visitors executed four birdies in succession and went back in front. Vardon got the birdie at No. 12, but Ray, in getting his par 4, produced this astonishing shot. His drive was the longest of the four, as usual, but right behind a tree. The tree was about forty feet in height, with thick foliage, and the ball was no more than the tree's altitude back of it, the tree exactly in line with the green. As Ray walked up to his ball, the more sophisticated members of the gallery were speculating as to whether he would essay to slice his shot around the obstacle to the green, 170 yards away, or "pull" around in on the other side. As for me, I didn't see anything he could do, possibly; but accept the penalty of a stroke into the fairway. He was out of luck, I was sure.

Big Ted took one look at the ball and another at the green, a fair iron-shot away, with the tree between. Then without hesitation he drew a mashie-niblick, and he hit that ball harder, I believe, than I ever have seen a ball hit since, knocking it down as if he would drive it through to China. Up flew a divot the size of Ted's ample foot. Up also came the ball, buzzing like a partridge from the prodigious spin imparted by that tremendous wallop—almost straight up it got, cleared that tree by several yards, and sailed on at the height of an office building, to drop on the green not far from the hole. . . . The gallery was in paroxysms. I remember how men pounded each other on the back, and crowed and cackled and shouted and clapped their hands. As for me, I didn't really believe it. A sort of wonder persists in my memory to this day. It was the greatest shot I ever saw.

Yet, when it was all over, there was old Harry, shooting par all that day and the next. And I couldn't forget that, either. Harry seemed to be playing something beside Stewart and Willie; something I couldn't see, which kept him serious and sort of far away from the gallery and his opponents and even from his big partner; he seemed to be playing against something or someone not in the match at all. . . . I couldn't understand it; but it seemed that way.

And that year, a bit later, I shot an 80 for the first time on the old course at East Lake.

I remember it with a peculiar distinctness. I was playing with Perry, and for once I wasn't bothering about what Perry was doing or if I was beating him or if he was beating me. I was scoring better than I ever had scored before and I couldn't think about anything else. And when I got down a four-foot putt on the last green for an even 80, which I never had done before, I made Perry sign my card and then I set off at a trot to find Dad. I knew he was on the course, and I ran clear across it, to the fourteenth green, and found him there. I had sense enough to wait until he was through putting; Dad was impatient of interruptions when he was putting. Then I walked up to him and held out the card. . . . I remember my hand was trembling a good deal. . . . Dad took it and looked at it and then he looked at me. I don't remember what he said. But suddenly he put his arms around me and hugged me—hard. And I do remember that his eyes looked sort of queer. I think now they must have been wet.

I suppose that is the first round I ever played against the

invisible opponent whose tangible form is the card and pencil; the toughest opponent of them all—Old Man Par.

. . . .

The year 1914 was on the immemorable side in golf for me, except that the new course at East Lake was put in play and I felt sort of lonesome for a while. I never had played anywhere else than on the old course, which was what is technically called a left-handed course—you traveled around it from left to right, as the hands of a clock, and I had some trouble getting used to the new course, which, like most modern designs, goes counter-clockwise most of the way. I never could understand why the clockwise course should be called left-handed, because it is the most unsuitable design for a left-handed golfer, since out-of-bounds is on the side to catch a left-hander's slice, and nearly all left-handers are gifted slicers. For that matter, most right-handers slice also, and should do better on what is called a left-handed course, where they might slice as far as they could without going out of bounds. At the time the East Lake course was changed that phase of it didn't affect me, as I was as likely to be off line one way as another.

At this period I was going to school regularly and had outgrown the habit of wading in puddles. I was playing more golf than tennis, as I had begun to suspect I could play golf better, but in the few club tournaments I got into my success was indifferent. I was regularly in either the second or the third flight and never seemed to win anything. Perry Adair and I played every Sunday, and I still watched Stewart Maiden play occasionally, simply from interest in his performance and with no idea of improving my own game or modeling it on his. . . . Stewart Maiden universally is termed my teacher, and the general idea is that Stewart started teaching me as soon as I was able to fall out of a cradle. This is quite wrong. Stewart never gave me a lesson in golf, though he has spent many hours, most of them profane, coaching me when I was in a slump with one club or another. I picked up my game watching him play, unconsciously as a monkey, and as imitatively. I grew up swinging so precisely like Stewart that when I was 15 years old and a chunky kid about Stewart's size and shape—I was playing in long pants in those days, as Stewart always has played—an old friend of Stewart's mistook me for him on the Roebuck Country Club course at Birmingham. I was playing in the southern amateur championship, or rather, I was playing a practice round before that tournament, and this man, who had not seen Stewart since he left Carnoustie, was standing by Dad as I was driving off the tenth tee in the distance.

"When did Stewart Maiden get here?" he inquired.

Dad told him Stewart was not there at all.

"You can't fool me," was the rejoinder. "I saw Stewart drive just now from the tenth tee. Think I don't know that old Carnoustie swing?"

"Nevertheless," Dad told him, "that happens to be my son Rob under that swing."

Stewart taught Alexa Stirling at the beginning of her golf career, and she too had "the old Carnoustie swing." Indeed, Alexa plays a good deal more like Stewart now than I do. I have changed some points of my swing, due to increasing anatomical differences—I am heavier than Stewart and wider across the shoulders and thicker in the chest. Perhaps in the head, too, as some of my alterations seem not to have worked out advantageously. In one regard, certainly, I went back two years ago to the old original Carnoustie style and got back my drive just when it seemed an attack of smothering and pulling would drive me crazy.

So I was still following Stewart around, and Stewart wasn't noticing me particularly, as far as I could see, though he did give me a tip once in a while, and made me a fine set of clubs as I outgrew the child-sizes. I acquired fancies in golf balls at this time. Earlier, a golf ball was a golf ball and nothing more. I never had played with the gutta-percha, or gutty, of course, and never had heard of it. The rubber-cored ball went on the market in 1902, the year I was born. The first ball I played with, after I began to notice that there were different kinds, was a Haskell Whiz; a fascinating ball marked with a little blue circle. I liked it a lot, and then, being fickle, I fancied the Dunlop Bramble and the Zome Zodiac, the latter name apparently hypnotizing me. . . . As late as 1916, the first year I played in a major championship, I was changing about frequently—sometimes in the same round. There was a big invitation tournament at East Lake, when it started raining the day before the tournament and rained steadily all through the event, and I was fond of the Black Circle ball then, a small and heavy and tightly wound ball with great distance (I believed), and against the wind on the wet turf I used the Black Circle, and with the wind I changed to a Black Domino; a big ball which sat up better in the soggy grass. I had ideas of golf ballistics in those days, or thought I had. . . . Those old balls, with the fancy names! All in the discard long ago—but I loved them devotedly in turn.

As to my progress the next year or two after making that epochal score of 80 on the old course at East Lake, my recollection is hazy. If indeed I was impressed with the importance of Old Man Par as a factor in golf, the impression was subjective and promptly overlaid by the more obvious features of the game. So far as I remember, I continued just playing, and trying to beat people, and butting into tournaments whenever I could manage it. I think I liked competitive golf a good deal better than I do now. All the last year I have been thinking what a wonderful thing it would be to reach the place where I could hang up my clubs and with them the obligations they entail, when used in major competitions. And yet, when I would see in the papers that the boys were assembling for the open or the amateur. . . . I don't know. An old warhorse at 25? Well, it looks a long, long way back to Merion in 1916.

I was beginning to read about golf in the papers at the time—in 1914—and I remember what an odd shock I got when I read that Chick Evans, playing at Sandwich in the British amateur championship, and favored to win, had been beaten by somebody named Macfarlane in what the account said was a "miracle round." Chick had played the first nine holes in 36, which was par, and was 5 down! I remember a sort of catch in my breath when I read that, and continued to read that Macfarlane had played the first nine holes in 31 strokes, including a bad 6 on a par 4 hole. I thought, what kind of golf is this? And what the dickens is there to do, if somebody shoots that kind of golf at you? . . . I have found out, more than once. Mostly, you take a licking as philosophically as possible. I've had enough of them to be somewhat philosophical about those I will get in the future. How Jess Sweetser did pour it to me, that first time at Brookline, starting with the mashie-niblick pitch he holed for an eagle 2 against my birdie 3, on the second hole! I was worse off than Chick at Sandwich—I was 6 down at the turn, though

I had not played as good golf as Chick. But I played well enough the next nine. I shot a 34—and gained back only one hole! Oh, the boys have poured it to me frequently! There was Max Marston, shooting five under par the last nineteen holes of our match at Flossmore in the national amateur. . . . But this is getting ahead of the story, and the first thing I know I'll be telling about young Andrew Jamieson, one of the finest kids I ever met, and how he stopped me in the British amateur championship, the day after I was pretty hot against Robert Harris, the British champion.

I must have been improving pretty fast through 1914, as the next year, when I was 13, I won two club championships and was allowed to play in the southern amateur championship and two big invitation tournaments away from home. The club championships came last, and the first big event of the year was the annual invitation tournament at Montgomery, Ala., always a great event in southern golfing circles. George Adair was taking Perry over there and he persuaded Dad to let me go along with them. Perry was going in great style by this time, and he and his father qualified in the first flight and met in the finals, Mr. Adair beating Perry and then going around looking as if he'd lost his last friend. Perry had beat him in the semi-final round of the southern championship the year before, but I think Mr. Adair didn't find revenge very sweet.

I didn't do so well in the medal round; it seems I had forgot all about the kick I got from that first 80 at East Lake. I qualified in the second flight, which disgusted me immensely. Probably I was pretty cocky in those days, and when I got to the final round of the second flight and was beaten by a man named Hickman who played left-handed, I wanted to throw my clubs in the river and give up the darned game. After getting into the second flight, it some way seemed adding insult to injury to be trimmed by a man who stood on the wrong side of the ball.

You see, golf still was just a game at which to beat someone. And of course I didn't know that the someone was myself.

CHAPTER THREE

FOURTEEN, AND A STATE CHAMPIONSHIP

DAD had told me he would let me enter the southern amateur championship when I was 15, provided I made sufficient progress, and it seemed I never was going to be 15, and the progress I made in the Montgomery invitation tournament certainly was not of a character to warrant me in making any impassioned plea this year—1915—despite the favoring circumstance that the southern was to be played at my home course, East Lake. So I was surprised and a little abashed when Dad told me I could enter it, and when I was named on the four-man team representing the Atlanta Athletic Club in the team match of the qualifying round, I was overwhelmed. The other members were Mr. George Adair and his son Perry, and Will Rowan, and I was so scared and burdened with responsibility in that round that I had to keep looking at the ground to keep from falling over. I seemed to be having a terrible round; but once more I was at grips with Old Man Par, and not thinking about beating anybody else, and I came in with a card of 83, the lowest score on our team and a single stroke back of the medalists, Nelson Whitney of New Orleans, the champion, and Charlie Dexter of Dallas, who tied at 82. . . . A card of 83—and it was called a great round in those days! I wasn't pleased with it, happy as I was to have helped my club's team win the match. I kept thinking of this shot I had pulled, and that putt I had missed. . . . It might so well have been an 80, or even better. But then, it's always so, in golf. Right now, thinking back to that stumbling old round in 1915 at East Lake, I can recall with not much more distinctness the first round at Sunningdale, qualifying last year for the British open championship, when I turned in a card of 66, and the critics next day said it was the finest medal round ever shot in Britain. Why, I remember a five-foot putt on the third green, that I missed for a birdie 3; and a simple ten-footer at the seventh; and another five-footer at the ninth, where I drove just over the green, 270 yards, and chipped back reasonably close, only to miss the putt. . . . I could have had a 63 there, as well as not. Or a 62. It's always so. It will be so, to the end of the chapter. You never have so good a round that afterward you can't see clearly where it might have been better. The lowest score I ever made on a full-sized course was a 63 at East Lake, September 16, 1922, just a week after Jess Sweetser had trimmed me at Brookline. The course is 6700 yards long and par is a fair 72. I had nine pars and nine birdies. And I could tell you right now of missed putts—I mean holeable putts—which would have given me a 60 at the worst. But I won't tell you. "The game is aye fetchin' ye," said one of the wisest of the old Scottish masters. And the game is aye on top, too—take it from me! No man ever will have golf under his thumb. No round ever will be so good it could not have been better. Perhaps that is why golf is the greatest of games. You are not playing a human adversary; you are playing a game. You are playing Old Man Par.

In those days they qualified 64 contestants in the southern, and the first round of match-play, at 18 holes, split the field into two divisions of 32, and the second round established the first, second, third and fourth flights. I met a chap named Patterson of Charlotte in the first round and defeated him, and then I encountered Commodore Heard of Houston, Tex., which made a match between the oldest and the youngest player in the field. The Commodore was, and is, a great figure in southern golf. I don't know how old he was then, but to me he seemed a lot older than I should like him now to think I thought he was, if you get what I mean. He was a short, stocky man with iron-gray hair and he wore a sun-helmet, and hit the ball with a short, flat swing that gave the ball a low flight and a tremendous run. I remember thinking, first, that he couldn't possibly keep the ball straight with that sort of poking swing, and next that he couldn't possibly get it *off* the proper line. And how he did putt! He didn't pay much attention to me, but when he closed me out on the seventeenth green, 2-1, he told me I was a tough customer and said I had made him shoot a 73 for seventeen holes to beat me. That afternoon he played Perry Adair and Perry beat him on the nineteenth hole, putting the ball on the green with his second shot, using a little spoon his father had had made for him at St. Andrews when they were touring the British golf courses the year before.

"Too many of these blamed kids," I heard the Commodore say, as he went back to the club house. Of course I was one of the kids, but it was Perry who beat him.

That match with the Commodore put me in the second flight and I met three men the shortest of whom was six feet two, beginning with Clarence Knowles, who was six feet three and weighed 220 pounds and was the longest driver in the South at the time. I must have made a funny contrast with these great musketeers—a stumpy, tow-headed schoolboy of 13, extremely red in the face, and playing golf in long pants because I was too proud of having assumed them to go back to knickers. One way and another, I beat all the big ones and met Frank Clarke of Nashville, in the finals, at 36 holes, and he did a 76 in the morning round, all putts being holed, which set a new amateur record for the course. He was 3 up at luncheon-time, and at the twenty-seventh hole he was 4 up. I then won the next four holes. Mother and Dad were in the gallery, and I was thinking how proud they must be of me, when I lost the next two holes. . . . I was thinking surely I had this bird, coming from behind to win four holes in a row and square the match; and it was a terrific jolt when he went right back into the lead again, with three holes to play. At the thirty-fourth I holed a chip-shot from off the green with an old mongrel Zenith iron, a great favorite with me, and was again in hopes, only to see him sink a 30-foot putt for the half. I was bunkered at the next green, got a half, and he closed me out, 2-1. I had shot a 78 approximately, and Mother and Dad said they were proud of me, but I didn't feel a bit proud of myself.

Here I was, 13 years old (I reflected), and, darn my time, I hadn't won anything yet! Only some little old junior championships and such. I felt that I was a disgrace to my family, and to Stewart Maiden, and to the Atlanta Athletic Club, and to anybody or anything else convenient to be disgraced. In long pants and Tech High School, and still hadn't won anything! I guess I moped about that southern championship more than I have brooded about anything since. It was almost as if I had expected to win the thing, with Charlie Dexter and Rube Bush and Nelson Whitney in it, and all. I wasn't much of a respecter of persons in those days, having few brains and no real experience. Golf was just a game, and if I couldn't hit one as far as Moose Knowles, why, I could stick a pitch against the pin and take up the slack, I considered. . . . It was on the nineteenth hole I beat Moose, the 220-pounder, in the southern. He out-drove me fifty yards and I couldn't reach the green with my second shot but I jammed a short pitch up by the hole and won the match.

My self-esteem still was several points off when Dad said I might enter the big invitation tournament at the Roebuck Country Club in Birmingham, and I'll always love Roebuck, because that was the first important tournament I won. I met Perry in the second round; the first of many times we met in formal competition in the next few years; and beat him, 2-1. Dad put up a heroic fight against Rube Bush of New Orleans, one of the most stylish players the South ever produced, and beat him in the same round. In the finals I met Bill Badham, a former Yale player, and we had a ding-dong match that went to the twenty-first green. . . . I remember thinking how blamed stubborn he was. I was shooting pretty good golf, but this fellow kept sticking and sticking and every time I made the least slip he won a hole from me. It seemed unreasonable, to me. . . . At the third extra hole I stuck a pitch shot stone dead and won.

This seems to have started me off on a sort of orgy of invitation tournaments and club championships. Dad was all excited over my winning at Roebuck, and the rest of that year and in 1916 I entered nearly every big invitation event in our section. I won the Davis and Freeman cup at East Lake, and the club championship there, in 1915, and won the Druid Hills club championship a bit later, breaking the course record with a 73 and winning a gold medal—my first—which I lost on the course the same year; employed two caddies to go over every shot I made in the round; found it where I had pulled to the rough at the fourth hole; lost it again, and never found it. In the finals of the 1915 club championship I played Archer Davidson, a huge chap and a powerful driver, but very lazy—I think he never had played 36 holes in one day before; and I beat him. . . . Looking over some old photographs the other day, I found a funny picture of Davy and me, taken after our match. Davy was about a foot taller than I, and I was grinning like a Cheshire cat. And under Davy's picture was scrawled in a schoolboy hand, "The Runner-Up," and under my picture, "The Champion." I was cocky, all right!

It seems I must have been interested in structural mechanics at this time, as in the same box was a set of three pictures, different views of a windmill about two feet in height, made from one of these toy construction outfits. And each photograph was painfully labeled, in the same schoolboy hand, "Windmill, Made By R. T. Jones, Jr."

So many people think I never did anything but play golf that I am glad to run across things to reassure myself that I wasn't altogether a dumb and predestined phenomenon.

In 1916 I started out with a rush of golf events and a prolonged attack of lumbago, which afflicted me soon after I played in the Montgomery invitation tournament, in the semi-finals meeting Perry Adair in the most spectacular of all the matches we played. I went out in 33 and was 3 up, and figured I had the match in hand. Then Perry broke away with a burst of golf that seldom can have been equalled. He came home in 33, including a stymie on the sixteenth green, and beat me on the last hole, 1 up. The little blond devil—they tell me he shot an even greater nine holes than that, coming from far behind to beat Frank Godchaux at Roebuck in the southern amateur championship of 1923. And he did shoot a 33 on a par 37 nine, and broke the course record. But I didn't see that, and what he showed me at Montgomery was sufficient. It was the hottest blast of really hot golf I had yet encountered; and I knew then why Perry was called the Kid Wonder of Dixie.

Dad continued a glutton for punishment and sent me up to Knoxville to play in the Cherokee Club's invitation, where I had lumbago so grievously that I had to walk down the hills sideways, and there were a lot of hills. I simply could not hit hard and as a consequence my drives remained in the fairway for the most part. . . . That was my trouble, in those days. I could pitch far better than I can now, and my irons were good enough. But I never could tell where my drives were going. As to putting, I was in a blissful state of abysmal ignorance concerning the difficulty of the game. Using a little, heavy, wooden-headed, center-shafted Travis putter, I banged the ball confidently at the hole from any distance and was furious over missing a fifteen-footer.... Lord—a few years later, when I had learned how hard putting really is, how I looked back in a sort of dumb misery at those earlier days! In 1920, and 1921, and 1922, I was thankful to get down a three-footer. As late as 1923 there was a short putt which left me in a tie with Bobby Cruickshank in the national open at Inwood. . . . But that's ahead of the story again.

I won the Cherokee invitation, shooting a 73 the last

round, and also won the Birmingham invitation, at the Country Club this time, shooting a 69 to defeat Jack Allison 2 up in the final round. It was at this tournament that I discovered that a hole in one shot, an achievement which has aroused a vast deal of conversation and publicity of late, was not necessarily a hall-mark of ability in golf. There was in the qualifying round of this tournament, a friend of mine, Webb Crawford, who made two holes-in-one in the same round, and finished with a score of 101. . . . I have played with many people who have made holes in one. I was playing with Walter Hagen when he made his only one, to date. I've made only one myself, in 1927, except those in the broad roadside ditch which served as Hole No. 2 for Frank Meador and me, on our first golf course. Which, naturally, do not count.

I won three invitation tournaments this year, defeating Perry in the finals of a tourney at East Lake when it rained all the time, and I used a little ball against the wind and a big ball with the wind, in spite of which I played pretty fair golf.

Then came the first Georgia state amateur championship, in August, at the Brookhaven course of the Capital City Club of Atlanta, and I suppose that's where I got headed for national competition. It was a pretty fast field, with Perry Adair and Simpson Dean as favorites among the younger generation, and some sterling veterans who fell by the wayside—it was terribly hot, I remember. I met Simpson Dean, a tall youth from Rome, later a famous player at Princeton, in the semi-final round and had him dormie 5 when he started a rally that rattled my teeth. He won the fourteenth, fifteenth and sixteenth holes in bewildering succession and on the seventeenth green he had a five-foot putt to win that one. He had the line exactly but the ball stopped one turn short. Gosh—he was disgusted!

"If I'd been three feet beyond!" he said, "I shouldn't mind. But to be *short*. . . ."

That brought Perry and me together, and we had what the papers called a classic struggle. Perry outplayed me in the morning round and I was 3 down at the intermission. I was furious with my putting, which for once was betraying me, and after a glass of milk and a sandwich I went out on the eighteenth green and chipped and putted for an hour, waiting for time to start—a terrible thing to do, but a kid can stand anything. Ralph Reed, chairman of the tournament committee, tells a good story about this incident. He says he went out and watched me and told me that a lot of the gallery had just arrived for the afternoon round, and asked me to play out the bye-holes, after the match was over—inferentially, after Perry had beat me. He says I said:

"Don't worry—there won't be any bye-holes!"

As I managed to beat Perry, 2 up, on the last green, this made a very fine story except that it is not in the least degree true.

I started out 3 down and shoved my second shot off into the woods on the first hole of the afternoon round and was 4 down. Then I got going and scraped out an approximated score of 70 with a 6 on the first hole. I got back the third hole with a birdie 3, we halved the next three in par figures, and I picked up the long seventh with a birdie 4. Perry really lost the match by missing a four-foot putt for a win at the eighth. I was under a strain I never was conscious of before, and I think if he had won that hole it would have settled me. As it was I got a half, turned 2 down, and Perry handed me the tenth, after which I battled along in par the rest of the way and won on the last green. It was the hardest match of the many Perry and I played, though not so spectacular as the one he beat me in Montgomery.

This performance got me the chance to enter my first national amateur championship, played that year at the great course of the Merion Cricket Club, near Philadelphia. Mr. Reed, who took a great interest in my play at Brookhaven, insisted I had earned the right to go, and Mr. Adair was taking Perry, so he took me along, too.

CHAPTER FOUR

BOUNCING BACK FROM A NATIONAL BOUT

MY début in national championship affairs at the Merion Cricket Club, Philadelphia, in 1916 has given rise to a deal of comment, due to my lack of years, and as the personal statistics have been somewhat mixed I may explain that I was 14 years and six months old, five feet four inches tall, and weighed 165 pounds—a chunky, rather knock-kneed, tow-headed youngster playing in long pants; supremely innocent of the vicissitudes of major tournament golf and the keenness of northern greens—so different from our heavy Bermuda texture in the South; pretty cocky, I suppose, from having at last won a real title, if only a state championship; and simply pop-eyed with excitement and interest. I had two weeks of violet-ray treatment for the lumbago that had tormented me earlier in the season, and it left me, never to return. I never had seen any of the great players who were to compete at Merion—Bob Gardner, then amateur champion, and Chick Evans, who had lately won the open championship at Minneapolis, and the others; and so far as I recall, I was not in the least afraid of any of them. I hadn't sense or experience enough to be afraid. Mr. Adair and Perry and I stayed at the Bellevue-Stratford hotel in Philadelphia and traveled out to the club on suburban trains. It was my first big trip away from home and I was having a grand time.

We played our first practice round on the West Course—there were, and are, two fine courses at Merion—and I never had seen any such beautiful greens. They looked like billiard tables to me and I was crazy to putt on them. But their speed was bewildering. I remember the sixth hole, then a short pitch down to the green over a brook, the green faced slightly toward the shot. I was thirty feet beyond the hole, which was in the middle of the green. Forgetting all about the faster pace of these new greens, I socked the ball firmly with my little Travis putter and was horrified to see it roll on past the hole, apparently gathering momentum, and trickle into the brook, so that I was playing 4 from the other side of the stream—a most embarrassing *contretemps.*

When the qualifying rounds came on, the field was divided into sections, one playing the morning round on the East Course, the other on the West Course, and both sections changing for the second round. I played the West Course in the morning and turned in a 74 which led the entire field for that round. After luncheon, when I got over to the East Course, word had got about that the new kid from Dixie was breaking up the tournament, and almost the entire gallery assembled to follow me. Gosh—it scared me to death! I fancy

I led the field the other way in the afternoon, taking an 89, for a total of 163, about ten strokes more than will get you in, these days, but safe enough then. Perry got in by a play-off at 167, won his first match, and lost the second. I was drawn with Eben Byers for my first match, a former national champion, and everybody in our party began to condole with me. Tough luck, they said, catching a big one in the first round. But Mr. Adair clapped me hard on the back and told me not to mind what they said.

"Remember what old Bob Fitzsimmons used to say," he advised. "'The bigger they are, the harder they fall!'"

I thought that was a corking line, but as a matter of fact the name of Eben Byers meant nothing to me. I was a fresh kid, and golf as yet didn't have me down—at least, I didn't know it.

Mr. Byers and I played terribly. He was a veteran and I was a youngster, but we expressed our feelings in exactly the same way—when we missed a shot, we threw the club away. This habit later got me no end of critical comment, some of which hurt my feelings deeply, as I continued reading references to my temper long after I had got it under control to where there was no outward evidence of it except my ears getting red, which they do to this day—for I still get as mad as ever, missing a simple shot.

These columns I've read about my temper—it seems I got off on the wrong foot, and it was a long time before I was anywhere near in step with the critics, in the matter of disposition and deportment. . . . Even now it strikes me as a bit unreasonable that so much type should have been employed on the gusty vagaries of one petulant youngster, when so little has been printed about the same unaffected displays by great golfers twice his age and more. There was only a whimsical reference to the club-throwing of Mr. Byers, I remember; and since then I have seen more than one national champion rival both of us. Two years ago at Oakmont, I saw a competitor in the national amateur championship heave his putter into an adjoining wood and forbid his caddy to go after it—and he has been a national title-holder more than once. But nothing was said about it in the papers.

I'm not saying I didn't need some lecturing, mind you. The golf writers have been only too good to me, all along. And I was a sort of bad boy of golf, I suppose, and required an occasional spanking, such as appeared in a Boston paper of 1918, when Alexa Sterling and Elaine Rosenthal and Perry Adair and I were playing a Red Cross benefit match at Brae Burn. I kept those spankings in my scrapbook, you see, along with the more pleasant clippings. This one was as follows:

"Some interesting golf was shown during the match, interspersed with some pranks by Jones, which will have to be corrected if this player expects to rank with the best in the country. Although Jones is only a boy, his display of temper when things went wrong did not appeal to the gallery."

That was two years after Merion. And I was a year or two more, getting my turbulent disposition in hand. It wasn't an easy matter. . . . It's sort of hard to explain, unless you play golf yourself, and have a temper. You see, I never lost my temper with an opponent. I was angry only with myself. It always seemed, and it seems today, such an utterly useless and idiotic thing to stand up to a perfectly simple shot, one that I *know* I can make a hundred times running without a miss—and then mess up the blamed thing, the one time I want to make it! And it's gone forever—an irrevocable crime, that stroke. . . . I think it was Stevenson who said that bad men and fools eventually got what was coming to them, but the fools first. And when you feel so extremely a fool, and a bad golfer to boot, what the deuce can you do, except throw the club away? . . . . Well, well—Chick Evans, writing years later, said I had conquered my temper not wisely but too well; that a flare now and then would help me. I liked that of Chick. But I could have told him I get just as mad today. I stopped club-throwing in public, but the lectures didn't stop coincidently. A bad name sticks. Having quoted one well-merited spanking, let me give an example of how hard it is to live down a wicked reputation.

Four years after Merion, and two years after Brae Burn, when I had reached the mature age of 18 years and the club-throwing penchant had been completely hammered out of me, I was playing in my first national open championship, at the Inverness Club, Toledo, qualifying with Harry Vardon. At the last hole I messed up a good round and took a villainous 6, finally missing a putt of about four feet. I was mad—thoroughly mad, certainly. But I didn't mean to show it. I holed out the ball, which lay at the edge of the cup, and tossed the putter to my caddy. He was not looking for it and the club fell on the green. Next day the newspapers said that I was throwing my clubs again, and had hacked up a slice of the eighteenth green in a rage after missing a short putt. . . . That hurt me a lot.

Well, well—I don't throw clubs any more, in public, though once in a while I let one fly, in a little friendly round with Dad and Chick Ridley and Tess Bradshaw—and get a deal of relief from it, too, if you want the truth.

Returning to my first match at Merion in 1916, after this bit of *apologia*—which may not be in the best of taste—I repeat that Mr. Byers and I played very wretchedly and I think the main reason I beat him was because he ran out of clubs first. Somebody playing behind us said later that we looked like a juggling act. At the twelfth hole Mr. Byers threw an iron out of bounds and wouldn't let his caddy go after it. I finally won, 3-1, and felt no elation whatever over my successful début in a national championship. I knew I was lucky to win, the way I had played, and that I ought to have been well drubbed.

The second match I played better. This was with Frank Dyer, champion of several states and districts, and he started fast, putting me 5 down in the first six holes. I was getting dizzy. "So this is big league golf," I reflected. Then Frank made a few mistakes and I saw he was human, and I began to play better. At the turn I was 3 down and when we stood on the eighteenth tee I had a 4 left for a 32 coming in, and was 1 up. I was shooting some hot golf and was enjoying myself immensely.

We both hooked from this tee and one ball stopped in a fairly convenient position on top of a mound while the other was at the foot of the same mound, in a distinctly distressing situation. We were playing the same kind of ball, a Red Honor. Mine had gone on an excursion out of bounds at the second hole and was wearing a tar-stain from the roadway; I didn't change the ball every sixth hole, as I do now, figuring that the one in play may be knocked slightly off-center. I didn't stop to examine and identify the balls, but confidently whaled away at the one under the mound and missed the shot grievously, taking a 6 and losing the hole. After holing out I looked at the balls, and discovered I had played his ball and he mine. There was nothing to do about it then—we had played out each with the wrong ball, and the score stood. We started the second round even, and I won, 4-2.

By this time the golf writers were paying me a good deal of

attention and some of the things they wrote made me feel extremely foolish. They wrote about my worn shoes and my dusty pants and my fresh young face and other embarrassing personal attributes. I never had considered my shoes or pants before, so long as they held together. Golf wasn't a dress-up game, to me, and it was a new and puzzling experience to be looked at closely by so many people. I never had thought much of my face, for example, and it seemed sort of indelicate thus to expose it in print, not to mention my pants. The galleries were the largest I had ever seen, of course, and only half a dozen familiar faces, but everybody was curiously friendly. . . . I remember thinking these Yankees must be pretty good folks, after all.

So I got through the second round and in the third round I met Robert A. Gardner, then champion, and the biggest gallery I had yet seen followed the match, which I will describe with some detail because of a certain significance it always has had, for me—it was in this match that I first got my fresh young head under the bludgeonings of chance, and, I must confess, wound up by bowing it.

Bob was playing with an infected finger, a handicap that rendered his game uncertain, and possibly cost him the championship in the end, as he lost to Chick Evans, who, however, was playing admirably in the finals.

I shot a 76 in the morning round and was 1 up. We were having a fine match, never far apart. In the afternoon we continued playing evenly and at the sixth tee we were square. When I planted my second shot on the green five yards from the pin I felt certain of going into the lead again, as Gardner's second was above the green and to the right, in a difficult place from which to approach. But he chipped stone dead and got a half.

At the next green my ball was fifteen feet below the cup and Bob's was off to the left. Again he chipped dead for a half.

I wasn't discouraged. He can't keep on doing it, I told myself. I'll get him yet!

Playing the eighth hole, my second shot was ten feet from the pin and Bob's was on the ninth tee—and this time he didn't chip dead. After his third shot he was still outside my position, and then I felt the break had come. He couldn't keep on doing it. The break had come. . . . But Gardner sank his twelve-foot putt, and I missed my ten-footer, and he had halved another. It seemed he *could* keep on doing it.

As for me, I couldn't. The break had come. But it was not my break. My fresh young head was bloody—and bowed. Frankly, I blew up. Bob won five of the next seven holes. He beat me, 5-3, holing a twenty-foot putt for a par of 4 at the fifteenth, after driving out of bounds.

They all told me it was a tough match to lose. But I've lost many a tough match since then, more than one by being clearly outplayed—and more than one because I simply blew up under pressure. And I've been out-finished in more than one medal-play championship. But I never have felt quite the same way again. In after years I began to reason the business out a bit; as I said early in these memoirs, I never learned anything from a match that I won; I got my golfing education from drubbings. And very lately I have come to a sort of Presbyterian attitude toward tournament golf; I can't get away from the idea of predestination.

The professionals, you know, have a way of saying of the winner in a competition, "It was *his* tournament." And step by step, and hole by hole, and shot by shot, you may trace it back and see that he was bound to win—after it is all over. . . . There's a tremendous lot to this game; and I fancied when I started this little story that maybe I could think a little of it out as I went along, and tell people about it. But it's a big assignment; too big for me. I may have reasoned out somewhat of the mechanical side; perhaps just a bit of the psychological side. But behind it all, and over it all, there is something I think nobody understands.

Anyway, as they said, this was a tough match to lose, because I had played very well up to the place where those continued recoveries of Bob's had broken my back, and next day one of the papers had a well-written account of the match which gave me a lot of credit and concluded with these lines:

"Carefree and unconcerned, save with the big dish of ice-cream awaiting him at the clubhouse, the Georgia schoolboy swung along from the fifteenth green in his worn shoes and dusty pants and sweat-streaked shirt, whistling an air from a recent musical comedy, as jaunty and complacent as if he had just won his first national championship instead of having just been beaten in the third round. He was thinking about the ice-cream."

But I wasn't. I was puzzled, and hurt, some way. Not with Bob Gardner, who had played so pluckily when his shots were not coming off, and had kept the pressure on, when I was hitting the ball better. Bob, as I recall it, was an abstract figure; he was in the picture only as an agent for something else, that I didn't understand. I had felt all along that I could beat Bob Gardner, but there was something besides him that was big and hard and invincible. . . . That was what kept the pressure on me; that was what beat me. Fatality wasn't even a word to me then; and it doesn't mean now what I want it to.

But as I walked back to the clubhouse—and I got the ice-cream, too—I kept wondering over and over again in a vague way what was on Bob Gardner's side, that had beat me, and made me blow up, when I was hitting the shots better than he was. Would it be on my side sometimes? I wondered. Or—with a queer little sinking sensation—would it always be on the other side?

You know, I never have made sure what it was, and is. I have found out this much: In the long run it seems to play no favorites—if the run is long enough. In my case it was a run of seven years.

CHAPTER FIVE

PROFESSIONALS, AND A RED CROSS TOUR

AFTER Merion and the national amateur championship of 1916, came the Big War, and if I carried away any introspections about golf from the beautiful course at Philadelphia, I lost them promptly in a singularly entrancing tour over a good deal of this my native land, playing what were called in those days Red Cross matches, and a flurry of War Relief matches, where the professionals were involved—my first experience in a normal way with the "pro" element which since has come to be so pleasant and fascinating a part of golf to me. . . . I love the professionals. I love to play with them and against them. I am perhaps inexcusably proud of the events in which I have been lucky enough to win from them; and, taking it the other way around, they have chastened my spirit with many and many a fine licking. The biggest golfing year of my life, 1926, began with the most impressive trouncing I ever got—and it was by a professional, Walter Hagen. I love to play against the pros, match or medal. A good deal has been written about my readiness to enter open events, when it was accepted that I had little or no chance to win—open tournaments in the Florida winter season—but I confess it was mainly selfishness on my part. Win or lose—what of it? I found there the spur of competition, and masters of the game who were all set to drub me—and usually did! Somewhere I read a line that sticks in my memory: "The fierce joy of conflict is the prize the vanquished gain!" I don't know about that fierce joy, but I do know I love to play against the professionals, and when I manage to beat them I am inordinately proud, and when they lick me, why, there's no sting in the defeat. . . . Well, not so much, I'd better say, to be honest. That licking Willie Macfarlane gave me in the play-off at Worcester, in the open championship of 1925, hit me pretty hard; but I can say honestly there was no sting in it. I did want to win that championship. Starting with a rotten round of 77, in thirty-sixth place—out of the championship, one newspaper asserted—I pulled up to tenth place in the second round; and fourth place in the third round; and a tie for first place in the fourth round. And then, with a lucky break, I tied Willie in the first play-off, and had him 4 strokes down with nine holes to play in the afternoon round. And he beat me. . . . I won't say it didn't hurt. It did. But a great round, and a great player, beat me. . . . Anyway, that's ahead of the story, which is away back in 1918, with the Red Cross matches.

No—wait a minute. In 1917 I won the southern amateur

championship, which was about the only fixture of any importance that got itself played in the first war-year. It was at Roebuck, in Birmingham, along in June, and I was then 15 years and three months old, if that is of any interest. It was my first sectional title. I beat Rube Bush, the New Orleans stylist—and a really fine golfer—in the fourth round and met Louis Jacoby, one of the best fellows and one of the most deliberate golfers I ever encountered, in the finals. I had Jake 4 down at the end of the morning round, and then, according to my stupid juvenile custom, I filled my system with pie *à la mode* at luncheon, toddled out on the course in a semi-comatose condition from a superabundance of calories, and proceeded to lose the first three holes of the afternoon round, cutting my lead to 1 up. The fourth hole at Roebuck was, and is, a neat iron shot from the tee and either I had assimilated some of the superfluous calories or had become aroused to the very perilous situation I was by that time occupying, for I laid a full iron shot of about 200 yards three inches from the hole, won it, and went on to win the match, 6-5, and the championship. . . . I'll never forget what Mr. Adair said, awarding the runner-up trophy to Jake. He told how, playing the long ninth hole, Jake was studying his second shot, a full wood, and taking plenty of time over it, as he did on most shots, and Mr. Adair heard one man in the gallery say to another:

"What's he waiting for?"

And the other, said Mr. Adair, replied:

"Oh, he's waiting for the grass to grow up under the ball and give him a better lie!"

So I won that tournament, and still I was just playing golf, and not learning anything about the game. I remember I had lost control of my pitches at Roebuck, and couldn't make them bite and sit down, so I just accepted it as a visitation of Providence or something and went on trying to chip back close enough to hole a putt.

I was a sort of champion, then, at 15, in the year 1917 when we were in the Big War, and J. A. Scott of the Wright & Ditson Company started booking Red Cross matches for us four kids—Alexa Stirling, Perry Adair and me, of Atlanta, and Elaine Rosenthal of Chicago. Mrs. Rosenthal chaperoned the girls; and Perry and I had the time of our young lives, traveling all over the eastern part of the United States, playing golf almost every day, and being acclaimed as fine young patriots—a phase of the tour which never seemed to register with me. I couldn't see that we were doing anything for our country. Simply playing golf, which was what we would rather be doing than anything else; visiting new golf courses—having a grand time. We played at New London and Boston and Holyoke and Ekwanok, and at Maplewood, up in New Hampshire; and Poland Spring, and Essex—lots of places. I was paired with Alexa one day and Elaine the next. . . . I remember Perry had a birthday at Ekwanok and got a pipe for a birthday present and smoked it; the first time he ever had smoked. Gosh—he was sick! And when I say sick, I mean sick as our British cousins mean sick, if you get what I mean. We were rooming at a little cottage, and Mr. Scott and I thought Perry was awfully funny. We jumped him from one bed to the other, trying to make him snap out of it. . . . I wasn't smoking then. I smoke a good deal now, and once in a while some golf writer takes a crack at me about it. When Walter Hagen was giving me that beautiful lacing in Florida, one scribe said he went around the course with 71 strokes and I with 75 cigarettes. Some people seem to think that's a bad idea. I don't know. I didn't smoke 75 cigarettes, of course. But I do light a good many, in a hard round. Light them, smoke them a bit, and throw them away. It's something to do, and seems to release a little of the tension. . . . It's easy to say cigarettes are bad for you. But what about that stretching and stretching and stretching, inside your head? It's easy to prove cigarettes are all wrong for you, physically. But championship golf is played mainly between the ears. If you don't smoke, I suppose you are better off—maybe. If you do smoke, I should say you were better off smoking, in a hard round. I noticed Ted Ray is never without his pipe; and old Harry Vardon smokes pretty continuously.

Perry and I were getting something of a reputation as the Dixie Kids, and a match was arranged at the Flossmoor Country Club, Chicago, for us to meet Chick Evans, then national amateur and open champion, and Bob Gardner, former amateur champion, who had beat me at Merion two years before. The two distinguished veterans were too much for us and gave us a good lacing. Later we played in Kansas City, and then, in St. Louis, Perry and I played Chick and Warren K. Wood, and finally beat them. . . . It was at St. Louis somebody gave Perry and me each a bright red Swiss Guard cap; a floppy affair, very snappy, we considered, and we wore them regularly in our matches thereafter. We played in Dallas and Houston and Fort Worth—I remember I shot a 70 and broke the course record there—and Galveston, and then home . . . . It was a joy ride for me. I had a world of fun. And when I heard that our combined efforts, mixed foursomes and all, had raised upwards of $150,000 for the Red Cross, I couldn't comprehend it at all. It had been so much fun!

I had been at home only a little while when I got a telegram from Chick Evans saying that Warren Wood, who was to have toured the East with him for the Red Cross, was ill, and asking me to take his place. I went at once to New York and met Chick, and we played two professionals, Jack Dowling and Tom McNamara, at Scarsdale and were beaten, 1 up, in a good match. We tried them again at North Shore and they beat us 2 up. We played pretty well but they teamed better. It's a big factor in fourball play. Chick and I scored the same on almost all the holes, while the pros were working so that one usually was having a shot for a birdie while the other played safe. That's the idea, in fourball play. That is why Harry Vardon and Ted Ray were such a grand fourball team. . . . I think Walter Hagen and I would do pretty well, as a fourball team. Our styles ought to dovetail admirably.

Then came the War Relief matches at Baltusrol, just out of Newark, N. J., and at Siwanoy, a New York course; and Garden City, Walter Travis' famous course, on Long Island. And here I became involved with the pros in earnest. Four teams were chosen—Amateurs, Homebred Pros, Scottish Pros, and English Pros. The play was in foursomes and singles. The first match was at Baltusrol, where the 1926 national amateur championship was played, and the amateurs had a distressing time of it. We played our foursomes against the English Pros, while the Homebreds fought it out with the Scottish Pros. Norman Maxwell and I were the only pair of amateurs able to count against our opponents, George Sargent and Herbert Strong, while Jerry Travers and Oswald Kirby, our No. 1 team, lost by the margin of a single hole to Gil Nicholls and Cyril Walker, and the rest of our outfit was unmercifully drubbed. I remember that Perry Adair and J. S. Worthington dropped four points to the Reid brothers, Wilfrid and Arthur.

In the afternoon we played the singles and here we did a

little better. Travers won three points from Gil Nicholls, and our No. 11 and No. 12 players, G. P. Tiffany and Robert Gwathmey, took three and five points respectively from H. Harris and Gordon Smith. I had a fine battle with Cyril Walker. He took the first three holes from me and then my temper came to my rescue. I didn't throw any clubs away but I suddenly got into a humor described by R. L. Stevenson in "The Master of Ballantrae" as "a contained and glowing fury." I won five of the next six holes of that crazy match, shooting 4-3-4-4-4-2, and Cyril, who was out in par 37, was 2 down at the turn. My fury cooled after I got ahead and I played only ordinary golf coming home, but Cyril was no better and I won, 1 up.

At the end of the first day's play the standing was: English, 44; Homebreds, 39; Scottish, 14; Amateurs, 13.

I was fortunate in all the singles matches, those three days we played against the professionals for the War Relief Fund, getting by without a defeat. At this distance I can see distinctly that I was extremely lucky; and in the foursomes I didn't do so well. Foursome play—each pair of partners playing alternate strokes with the same ball—was a new thing for Perry and me and we had some curious rounds and one dreadful drubbing. But we enjoyed the foursomes, winning or losing. At Siwanoy, on the second day, we played against George Simpson and Alex Cunningham, and neither side was shooting good golf. Alex and I had much the same sort of temper. Alex was playing badly and George was kidding him, and along about the fifteenth hole he missed a putt of about eighteen inches and threw his putter at least a hundred yards into some trees. It was the longest club-throw I had ever seen.

Next day at Garden City Perry and I played Jack Dowling

and Emmett French, and our side was having a fearful time, mainly due to my bad play. Perry would drive down the fairway and I would fire the ball out into the rough, and poor little Perry would get it back on the course and then I would shoot into a bunker. Sometimes we varied the procedure by Perry driving into the rough on one side and me hitting clear across into the rough at the other side. Garden City is no course for that type of play and we were deservedly licked, 8-7, in an 18-hole match.

I encountered just a bit of the psychology of golf when Perry and I played with two professionals just before the set War Relief matches, meeting Jack Hobens and Nipper Campbell in a 36-hole medal competition at Englewood. I was feeling pretty cocky and led off with a 3 at the first hole and a 3 at the second—both par 4 holes.

"Well, Bobby," said Jack, "eighteen 3's make 54, you know."

I never hit another shot, as I recall it, and finished with a wretched 80. Isn't that odd? Just got to thinking about making 3's, and it was 5's and 6's from then on.

Chick Evans and I played Johnny Anderson and Jerry Travers at New Britain, and we won, 5-3. I had a 71, which was the best card. You see, I recall my good cards, which were not so numerous. Chick and I also beat Anderson and Max Marston at Baltusrol. I wish I knew how many matches I played in 1918. It was a lively year for me. But I was just a kid of 16, having a huge time, and proud of my red Swiss Guard cap and the occasional flattering notices about me in the papers, and I didn't even bother to keep a scrap-book of the various tours. A few scattered clippings; a picture or two—and the red Swiss Guard cap; they are all I have. And the memories. Best of all I remember how I enjoyed battling with the professionals.

And that is about all the statistics this humble narrative will contain. It was an eventful era, though not in the way of championships or important tournaments. With the year 1919 we enter the arena in earnest.

I always think of 1919 as my runner-up year. I was only a semi-finalist in the southern amateur championship, played at New Orleans with a crafty design the last week before national prohibition set in; Nelson Whitney defeated me handily, 6-5, after I had held him level the first 18 holes, and went on to win in the last round from Louis Jacoby. Then I entered the Canadian open championship—a bad year for everybody to enter it but the late Douglas Edgar, that strange and fascinating little Englishman who came to the Druid Hills Golf Club that spring and won the Canadian with the lowest score ever recorded for a national open championship in any country. He had rounds of 72-71-69-66—278, and he was just sixteen strokes ahead of Jim Barnes, Karl Keffer and myself, who were tied for second place with 294, a decent and respectable score on the Hamilton course. . . . I took three putts on the 72nd green and lost my chance for an unadulterated second place. . . . What a round that 66 was! I watched most of it, and Douglas was simply playing tricks with the ball, bending it out of bounds to make it come in with a great run toward the green on a dogleg hole; that sort of thing. His approaching was so good that on one green only he had a putt of more than a dozen feet. This was at No. 12, a hole of 300 yards, where he drove the green and missed a long putt for an eagle 2. The gallery concluded he had blown up.

I went home to Atlanta and was second to Jim Barnes in the southern open championship on my own course, East Lake, and it was in the second day's play that I got a sharp taste of golf when you are shooting par and it doesn't help you any. We were playing together, in the third round, and I was going along in par when Jim touched off some fireworks. Beginning at the fourth hole, par was 5-5-3 through the sixth and that is exactly what I scored. And I lost four strokes to Long Jim. He had a birdie 4 at the fourth. He then pulled his drive far into the rough on the 600-yard fifth hole, pushed a brassie clear across the fairway into the rough on the other side, and then holed out a mashie shot of 150 yards for an eagle 3, while I was plugging along for a par 5. After that he stuck his iron drive on the Island green, three yards from the pin, and canned the putt for a deuce, while all I could do was a par 3. I was getting discouraged when in some way he managed to take a par 4 at the seventh, and the gallery, seeing him miss a putt of five yards for a birdie 3, decided he was exploding. . . . He didn't explode. Not that round. I nearly caught him, in the afternoon, but he finished a stroke ahead on the 72 holes and I was runner-up again.

And then I was runner-up at the Oakmont Country Club, Pittsburgh, in the second national amateur championship in which I had played. I was pretty lucky in that tournament, even so, because I never was on my game, and might as well have lost in any of the first three rounds. At any rate I got to the finals with Davy Herron, an Oakmont player then, and he gave me a good drubbing in a match with an incident about which a good many columns have been written. I never could figure that incident as beating me, but it did shut off the last rally I had in my system. Still, I was 3 down at the time, with seven holes to play, and even had I won the long twelfth hole, I would have been 2 down and six to play. They said—some of them—that I might have pulled the match out, even so, but for that megaphone. But I don't know. You remember, I told you it looks more and more as if this game is all in the book before a ball is hit; and you merely go through a championship tournament as you were rehearsed to go through it, perhaps a million years before. That sounds thoroughly idiotic. Well, maybe you weren't rehearsed. Maybe you simply play a tournament like one of the Tony Sarg marionettes, with somebody over you pulling the strings. . . . I wonder who held the strings attached to that man with the megaphone.

CHAPTER SIX

RUNNER-UP AT OAKMONT

OAKMONT, in the pretty hills outside of Pittsburgh, in August of 1919, was the scene of the most impressive hailstorm I ever saw on a golf course and the highest crop of qualifying scores of any national amateur championship I ever took part in. They had an odd system at Oakmont, too, in 1919. The field played one round on Saturday to reduce the number of competitors to 64 and ties, and the survivors played 36 holes Monday, to qualify 32. The hailstorm came along on Saturday. I remember Francis Ouimet took an 8 on the last hole, trying to putt over hailstones. There was no hail Monday, but the scores went upward just the same. S. Davidson Herron, the ultimate winner, was tied for the medalist's position at 158 with Jimmy Manion and Paul Tewkesbury. I had 159 and was the only other competitor under 160. The qualifying scores went all the way up to 172, or two average rounds of 86. It was, and is, a severe golf course, Oakmont. I think it's the best test of championship golf in this country.

Now, however popular opinion may have it, my clearest recollection of the championship of 1919 is not the licking I got from Davy Herron in the finals, though I remember it quite clearly enough. It is the amazing battle between those classic rivals, Chick Evans and Francis Ouimet, who were to meet again the next year at Roslyn, with a different result. Both Francis and Chick were ill, at Oakmont. Chick was suffering severely from rheumatism and Francis had a fever and could eat nothing but orange juice, and they got together in the second round and the weather was unfavorable to both. So each of them got around that tremendous course in a stroke better than par, 73 each, as I remember it, and they were all square in the morning round. Bob Gardner and I, starting off first, managed to get our match over rather early and I saw part of the afternoon round between Chick and Francis.

The first nine holes simply had me gasping. Starting all square in the afternoon, Francis went out in 34 with a bad 6 on No. 9, and had Chick only 1 down, Chick having gone out in 35. Both were better than par for the 27 holes they had played, on one of the longest and finest courses in the world.

Human machinery couldn't stand it, and both collapsed on the finishing nine—it is not surprising. They played loosely, and Chick finally picked up the single hole he was down and at the thirty-sixth tee they were all square. I was pop-eyed with interest and excitement; it was a battle of giants, to me.

They got good enough drives, but Chick's second was in the bunker at the right. Then Francis' second found a bunker, at the left. Chick played a good recovery, ten feet past the hole, and Francis got just inside of him, about nine feet to the left. Chick studied the putt carefully and missed it, and Francis got his putt down for the match. . . . He lost next day to Woody Platt, in a grim struggle that went to the thirty-eighth green.

I wasn't playing at all well, but was consistently lucky up to my final match, where I was outplayed, anyway. I defeated Manion, 3-2; Bob Gardner, 5-4—thus getting some revenge for the 5-3 spanking he had given me in the previous championship; Rudolph Knepper, 3-2; and W. C. Fownes, Jr., 5-4. Davy Herron meanwhile was really earning his way through the other bracket, and winning all but one of his matches by wide margins. We got together in the final round and I was playing better than at any time previous in the tournament. We were square at the end of the morning round. In the afternoon, Davy began sinking long putts, and as we stood on the twelfth tee I was 3 down with 7 holes left to play.

It was on this hole, which is a gigantic affair of more than 600 yards, that the megaphone incident took place, and I want very much to make it plain that my defeat in the match and my loss of the championship ought by no means to be charged to that incident. I believe with all my heart that Davy would have beaten me anyway. Yet there is no use denying that the megaphone *did* affect the play on the long twelfth hole, and I want also to employ the incident as a little object-lesson for gallery officials.

I was 3 down, then, on the twelfth tee, and I had a better drive than Davy, who was bunkered and got an indifferent recovery shot for his second. I was at the top of my swing for a full brassie, designed (as I hoped) to land the ball near or on the green, when a gallery official, seeing part of the gallery in motion, roared, "Fore!" through his megaphone.

Of course he was watching the gallery instead of me. And, equally of course, he intended to stop the gallery-motion and give me a fair chance at the shot. But the motion of the gallery was not bothering me in the least. What ruined me was that shattering shout of "Fore!" just as I was coming on the ball. . . . I flinched, hit the ball on the roof, and topped it into a bunker; failed on my recovery, and picked up. Where I might have been only 2 down, I was now 4 down, with six to play. . . . As I say, I feel sure Davy would have beaten me anyway; he was playing the best golf of the field. But there was something about that megaphone blast that seemed to tell me, as clearly as I suppose the Angel Gabriel will call time on us one day, that this was not my turn. . . . That's partly what I mean when I suggest that a golf tournament is all in the book, before a ball is driven. . . . I've missed shots in a pinch; I've seen many an opponent hole a long putt, or make a great recovery, in a crisis most embarrassing to me—just as Bob Gardner did, in giving me that first licking, at Merion. But nothing ever announced to me as distinctly as that megaphone that I was beaten. I was beaten, all right, and it ended two holes later, 5-4.

Now the little object lesson on megaphones, if I may presume so far.

I wish all gallery officials realized, as all tournament golfers do, that the megaphone is the most alarming hazard that ever appears on a golf course. The gallery becomes almost a part of the course and part of the round, to the experienced competitor; either he can play with a gallery following him, or he can't—and if he can't, of course, the gallery doesn't follow him. The gallery is like any other hazard. Sometimes it even is a help, as putting on a windy day, when several thousand people are standing massed about the green. Usually it does not help, however. At Columbus last year in the open championship, I turned away from my ball three different times, preparing to drive from the tenth tee, when spectators went scurrying, rabbit-like, across the fairway a hundred yards ahead. Then I missed the shot farther than I missed any other drive of the tournament. The gallery is harder on the pair immediately behind, than on the pair it is watching. Most spectators seem to have no idea there is any other match or pair on the course. And that is the main trouble with the megaphone official. If he is experienced enough and careful enough not to bellow when one of his own pair is about to play, he is likely to shout at the gallery when some competitor in another match, perhaps on a parallel fairway not fifty yards away, or on a nearby green, is executing a stroke. . . . And it doesn't matter what the reason is, or how excellent the motive—the fact remains that of all things against which no golfer can steel himself, the shattering blast of a megaphone stands out as the main stroke-wrecker. The experienced tournament competitor can guard himself against gallery motion, by simply not playing, if the motion is in his range of vision. But he cannot protect himself against the megaphone, in his own gallery, or in any other gallery within earshot. . . . I like the flag system best; and the quiet and dignified "Stand!" in the unaided human voice, that does not go echoing across the course as if delivered by the Bull of Bashan, to devastate some distant competitor. When galleries number up to, and above, fifteen thousand persons, as they frequently do these days, they are bound to be a problem. But I never shall believe the megaphone is the solution. . . . When there is a megaphone in my gallery, I spend a lot of my time watching the man with it.

A deal of fun has been poked at golfers for being sensitive to sudden noises and sudden motion when playing a stroke.

People ask me why we aren't like baseball players and football players, unaffected by shouts and such things. This is not hard to explain. If the gallery were confined in a grandstand, and keeping up a continuous clamor, the golfer could concentrate about as well as if all were quiet and orderly. Golf is not a game of rapid action, like baseball. Where a moving ball, or a moving opponent, is the objective, other motions and extraneous sounds have little or no distracting influence. But in golf, as I heard one man—an Englishman—express it once, the player is all alone with his God and the shot. Not a poor idea. He *is* all alone, though twenty thousand spectators may be massed about him. Only *he* can play that shot, on that ball, perfectly at rest. And I can say with all reverence that only God can know what some shots cost a golfer. That Englishman had an idea.

Well, well—that long twelfth hole which saw me well trounced at Oakmont in 1919 was the turning point of one of the hardest matches I ever played, six years later, when I was in the final round with Watts Gunn. . . . You know, this curious destiny that shapes our ends actually does seem to play no favorites, in the long run—if the run is long enough. . . .

The golf writers called it the Ghost Hole, that No. 12 at Oakmont, when I went there in 1925 to play again for the championship. They wondered if a gray ghost of that old, old mishap (they called it a tragedy) would haunt me and touch my nerve, in the 1925 championship. . . . And I was 1 down to Watts Gunn in the first round of the final match, and going to the twelfth hole—the Ghost Hole—I was trapped with my third, and Watts was well on the green. I'll always believe if Watts had won that hole, he'd have won the championship. We'll get to that in due course.

So I was runner-up at Oakmont, in 1919, and now the

tournaments are piling up and I'll have to try to pick out just a spot here and there; I hate statistics. And if you fancy this little story is too much about me, I beg you to remember that all my life I've been playing in tournaments and that I've seen precious few in which I was not a competitor. Which makes a difference in the way you regard tournaments, just as you are bound to consider a golfer rather differently, when you are trying to beat him instead of merely watching him.

I lost eighteen pounds in the Oakmont championship. This may be news to the sport writers who still fancy golf is an easy, old man's game which takes nothing out of you. I always lose from ten to fifteen pounds in a championship of three or six days' duration. It can't be the physical strain. I can play 36 holes of golf every day for two weeks and weigh the same at the end. In a championship the fire seems to be hotter. There are two kinds of golf: golf—and tournament golf. And they are not at all the same thing.

In 1920, I had a figure. From a chunky boy of 14 I had grown six inches and lost twenty pounds, and my waistline—I wish I had it today. I was almost slender, in 1920, when I went to Chattanooga with a large and lively delegation from Atlanta and won the southern amateur championship. I was playing fairly well and was not much pressed in any match, and my success impelled certain friends to urge my entry in the western amateur championship at Memphis the next week. So I went over there and qualified in rounds of 69 and 70, then a western record in those simple and straightforward days.

Perry Adair and Tom Prescott of Atlanta were in the Dixie delegation, and with them and Pollack Boyd of Chattanooga, and myself, a four-man team was made up to represent the southern golf association in the Olympic Cup match, the first qualifying day. We won it. It was the biggest cup I ever saw until the international matches started with Great Britain a couple of years later at Southampton, L. I., and I got a sight of the Walker Cup.

I thought I had a good chance to win the western amateur title but Chick Evans stopped me, as he had a habit of stopping anyone who fancied he could win it. I got through the first three rounds in fine style, playing very good golf at the Memphis Country Club—a neat course—and then I met Chick. We had one of the greatest matches I ever took part in, and I want to say that the way he beat me proved, to my mind, that Chick is one of the gamest and best competitive golfers the world ever saw. He had me 3 down in the second round, with seven holes to play, and then I got a crazy streak and took those three holes back in succession, two of them by sticking an approach shot stone dead. We were square, and I thought I had him, sure. The hardest thing in golf is to see a good lead cut away fast, and still play your game. . . . I wish I could give you all the details of that match; how we sparred like two boxers, and how Chick judged from my caddy's demeanor—he was a smart caddy and a pugilist—that I had a good second shot at one hole, and so Chick went for an almost impossible shot over a tree, when in reality I was away off in the woods. And how we each sank an eight-foot putt at the thirty-fourth, and how I thought I had him licked at the thirty-fifth, when his second was in a deep grass trap and mine was on the green. He beat me there. My approach putt was wide and left me a six-footer, while he came out of the trap a dozen feet from the pin and sank the putt for a par 4. I'll never understand my own putt, which hit the cup, ran clear around it, and came out on the same side as I was, and looked me in the eyes, and said: "You're licked!" I was licked, sure enough. Chick outfinished me. And I thought I had him. He beat Clarence Wolff next day in the finals.

I suppose the main event of this year was my first entry in the United States open championship, played at the Inverness Club, Toledo, August 10-13. I played typical kid golf on a fine course, and when I had a chance to win I didn't know it; I didn't know then that the universal tendency is to blow up in the fourth round, if you haven't already blown up in the third. I got going in the third round and shot a 70. Harry Vardon, fifty years old, was leading the field with 218 for the three rounds; Hutchison and Leo Diegel had 219; Ted Ray was 220; I was 222, and Chick Evans was 223. Gosh—I actually had a chance! I studied the score board, ate a hearty luncheon of pie and ice-cream, and decided I needed another neat little 70, or better, to win. I started badly, thinking about that 70, tried foolish and desperate shots, and finished stupidly with a 77. . . . I didn't suspect that everybody else was going to blow up in the last round. Gee—a 72 would have won for me! But I was full of pie and ice-cream and inexperience, and finished in a tie for eighth place with Willie Macfarlane who five years later was to beat me in a play-off in the national open at Worcester.

They all blew up, in the fourth round—Vardon, and Ray, and the Hutch and Diegel. Ray blew up least; he took a 75 and won. Chick Evans kept trying, shot a 75, and nosed me out of the leading amateur's place by one stroke. What a tournament that was!

A curious fatality—more food for thought among any who have a fancy of predestination in golf championships—kept Harry Vardon from winning the title when he seemed to have it in the bag, and the incredible distinction of winning the American championship twice, twenty years apart; he won it in 1900.

With the last nine holes to play Vardon was leading the field by four strokes and picked up another at the eleventh. He seemed sure to win; it was "his tournament," as the professionals say. But as he stood on the twelfth tee, facing the longest hole of the round, a sudden gale whipped up in his face out of a black sky. The grand old boy was tiring fast. He hit the ball hard and accurately, but against the gale it took him four shots to reach the green. He lost a stroke; lost another at the next hole; the wind died away in a few minutes, but Vardon was spent. He lost six strokes on the last seven holes and finished in a tie with Jack Burke at 296. What a finish that was! Ted Ray came along with 295 and went out in front. Then came Jock Hutchison, and then Leo Diegel, with Chick Evans carrying his clubs, and each had a long putt on the last green to tie Ted Ray—and missed. . . . I remember Walter Hagen, several strokes behind, was playing with the Hutch, and Walter, from the edge of the green, sank a long one for a birdie 3. He threw back his black head and laughed as the gallery of ten thousand roared.

"I wish you had it, Jock," he said.

Then Jock, his face twisted with the strain, putted and missed his chance at glory.

Diegel missed a fifteen-footer at the seventy-first green as well as one nearly twice as long at the last hole, to tie for the lead. Four men were tied for second place, Vardon, Burke, Hutchison and Diegel, one single stroke back of the victor. With a score of 299 and that last bad round I was only four strokes back. . . . A fourth round of 72 would have won me the first open championship in which I played, and doubtless would have ruined me utterly. Of all the luck I've had, and I've had a lot, the best luck is that I didn't win at Merion as a kid of 14 in my first amateur championship, or at Inverness, in my first open. . . . But that tremendous finish at Inverness hypnotized me. Think of it—five players having a chance to win, right up to the seventy-second green! I concluded right there that the open championship was the thing. . . . I confess it still is my idea of a tournament. . . . I watched Leo Diegel play the last three holes, and I remember wondering why his face was so gray and sort of fallen in. . . . I found out, for myself, later.

Harry Vardon and Bobby Jones at Bobby's first national open championship at Toledo in 1920.

CHAPTER SEVEN

THE FIRST BRITISH VENTURE

HARRY Vardon's first comment on my golf was at the national open championship in 1920, at Toledo, and I still regard it as the funniest and most conclusive estimate I ever heard on anything. By some happy circumstance I was paired with Vardon, the Old Master, for the two qualifying rounds. I was delighted and more than a little flustered—Harry Vardon had been a hero and an idol to me ever since I first saw him play, when I was a kid 11 years old, at my home course in Atlanta.

Harry and I were tied at the end of the first round at 76, I think, and in the second round I was doing a little better. We came to the seventh hole, a dogleg, with the drive over a yawning chasm and some tall trees, if the bold player would go straight for the green. Ted Ray really won the championship on this hole. It was a good par 4 and Ted got a 3 in each of the four rounds, being twice on the green with his drive, a punch of about 275 yards.

Harry and I took the big jump safely and were in front of the green, each with a short, plain little shot to get near the flag. Harry was a bit farther away and played a simple run-up, not far from the pin. In those days I loved to pitch, and elected to use a niblick, though there was no intervening trouble. I looked up on the shot and committed the most horrid mistake possible under the circumstances; I topped the ball and it scuttled like a rabbit straight over the green into a bunker. . . . To this day my ears get hot, thinking of that shot.

I played out for a bad 5, losing a stroke to par, and, desperately embarrassed, walked on to the next tee with Harry, who had not said a word thus far in the round. I thought I would ease my own embarrassment and break the ice at the same time. So I said:

"Mr. Vardon, did you ever see a worse shot than that?"

He said:

"No."

This appeared to close the incident.

Less than a month later I went to the national amateur championship at the Engineers Club, near Roslyn, Long Island, and that was the last of the lighthearted and carefree entertainment's golf has served me in what they call the Big Show. After that, the matter became increasingly serious.

But in September, 1920, I was 18 years old, still addicted to pie *à la mode* between rounds, and still playing, or endeavoring to play, tournament golf just as I played other golf. This was my third national amateur tournament, and here and there people were beginning to wonder when I would break through and win one. I was acquiring a reputation, you see, with state and sectional championships and Red Cross matches and the like. My Dad was convinced that I was good enough to win a national title, and made no bones about telling me so. All of which got me to thinking about it myself, in a different way than before, when a golf tournament was simply a golf tournament, and the bigger the better. Dad was not with me at Philadelphia in 1916, or at Toledo, in 1920. But he went with me to Oakmont in 1919, and to the Engineers Club in 1920, and I could see he was greatly set on my winning.

Chick Evans was the man of destiny at the Engineers Club and he won the championship, playing against Francis Ouimet in the finals the best golf I have ever seen in our national amateur event. But to reach the final round. . . . Now let me just tell you about this.

Chick won his first match easily and met Reginald Lewis in the second round. Reggie was playing strong golf and Chick had not yet come on his game, and going to the thirty-sixth hole Chick was one down.

One down, and one to play—Chick had to win that hole or be out of the tournament.

From the tee Chick pulled to a bunker, and his second shot was a hundred yards short of the green and in deep clover; perhaps the most difficult thing out of which to play a pitch shot with "stop" on it. Reggie's second was just over the green on a slope; a fairly simple chip from the hole.

Chick by a great pitch got his ball on the green, five yards from the pin, but he had played 3 and Lewis needed only a half to close him out. Lewis took some time studying his chip-shot and Chick was so nervous he could not stand still. He walked off to one side of the green and paced back and forth, out of Reggie's vision, of course. Reggie played a fair chip; his ball was closer than Chick's, but not dead by any means. Chick had a mean, sidehill, curving putt of fifteen feet and he had to sink it, and Lewis had to miss a shorter one, if Chick were to keep the match alive. . . . Well, Chick sank his putt, and tottered off the green, and dropped on the turf, waiting for Reggie Lewis and fate to settle the business. . . . Reggie missed. The match went into extra holes. Lewis had another putt to win at the thirty-seventh green, and the ball was in the cup—but it switched out. Both were groggy. Chick finally won on the forty-first green; the longest match of my observation in the national championship. He was that near being out, in the second round. And then he went on to win the title, with never another close match.

Tell me there isn't destiny in golf!

I think I never enjoyed a match more than mine with Freddie Wright in the third round of that tournament. Freddie and I were about the same age, and we had tied at 154 for the medalist's position and agreed to let the medal ride on our match, if we got together, which we did. We also seemed to have agreed to shoot 3's exclusively, if possible. Freddie shot a birdie 3 at me on the first hole, where I took a sorry 5. I countered with a 3 at the second. We halved the third in par 4, and Freddie nicked me with another 3 at the next. In some way I won the fifth hole with a conservative 4, and then fired three 3's at Freddie in succession. He reached the turn in 35, which was par, and was 2 down. I had eight 3's in the morning round, and the match ended at the short fourteenth hole in the afternoon, the famous "2-or-20," where I stuck a niblick pitch from the tee a foot from the cup for a deuce. . . . It was a corrugated niblick, that club, and the only one I ever could really pitch with. I can't use it now. It's illegal, under the ruling of 1922.

I had won by rather wide margins from my old friends Simpson Dean and Frank Dyer, and this victory put me in the semi-final round with Francis Ouimet, who chastened my ebullient young spirit with a good spanking, 6-5. . . . It was my last trouncing as a kid, though I have had many since then. . . . I was 3 down at the end of the morning round, missing a putt of two feet on the last green, which didn't help my youthful conceit of myself, and in the afternoon I simply could not close the gap. Francis was playing good golf and we had the biggest gallery I had ever seen. . . . I suppose it was at the seventh green of the afternoon round that the kid-spirit cropped out for the last time.

Each of us was on the green with the second shot, and I was a bit outside, but with an easier approach putt, slightly uphill. Francis was solemn as a judge; he always is, in a match. As I was preparing to putt a bee came buzzing along and alighted on the ball. I shooed it away. It returned at once. I shooed it away again. It then took up a position on the green nearby, and a gallery official popped his megaphone down on the persistent insect, which instantly emerged from the mouthpiece and came back to me—it seemed to be fond of me. The gallery was beginning to giggle. I took off my cap and chased that pertinacious bee clear off the green. I got to laughing myself, and the gallery fairly whooped. I think even Francis smiled a little, but I'm not sure.

Having disposed of the bee, I went back to the ball myself, made a wretched putt, and failed to sink the next one, losing the hole. . . . Sometimes I fancy that bee flew away with a good bit of my juvenile fancy for the game of golf. Anyway, it hasn't seemed the same since the Engineers Club in 1920.

Francis stopped me at the thirteenth green in the afternoon round and the gallery did one of the prettiest things I can remember. He was an easterner, immensely popular then, as he is now; I was a southerner, still with a reputation for petulance. But when I walked through a lane in the huge gallery about the thirteenth green, where everybody, including myself, knew I was to get the *coup-de-grâce*, there was a wonderful crackle of applause, that made my eyes sting suddenly. It was a kindly and gracious tribute I shall never forget. I began right there to love golf galleries. . . . Some of them in their eagerness have knocked me about a good deal, since then. More than once I've been knocked flat in the rush. But I still love them.

Dad was pretty well broken up over my defeat. I felt worse about him than on my own account. They gave me a flag next day and made me one of the stewards, so I could watch the final match between Francis and Chick, but I couldn't see much of it. The gallery was estimated at thirteen thousand. I didn't use my flag much for fear I might get killed. But I saw some great golf. From the tenth hole in the morning round through the tenth in the afternoon round, Chick used 71 strokes for nineteen holes, as I recall it. . . . That tournament saw a British invasion of our amateur championship—Cyril Tolley, Lord Charles Hope and Roger Wethered. None of them qualified. Strange conditions and that short tenth hole seemed to beat them. I was sorry. I met them all and have seen much of them since, especially Cyril and Roger, and got to be very fond of them.

After the championship I played in an invitation tournament at the Morris County Country Club and won it—it seemed I could win the little ones but not the big ones. Then Chick Evans and I played Vardon and Ray and gave that celebrated pair the worst beating they ever got, I suppose; 10-9. I was good in the morning and Chick in the afternoon; he had three 3's in succession on par four holes in the first nine; and Harry and Ted were worn out from a long tour; they were about starting back home. Oswald Kirkby and I beat them an 18-hole match one morning at Englewood, and Cyril Walker and I beat them again in the afternoon, due mainly to the excellent playing of my partners. . . . The old boys were pretty tired. But I didn't get very cocky about those fourball matches. I remembered Ray had won our open championship and Vardon was second—when it counted. Matches were one thing. The open championship was another.

Now we must cover a lot of beautiful territory rapidly, as I went to Great Britain the following early summer, in 1921, and added a lot to my meager stock of golfing education by taking a lacing in the British amateur championship at Hoylake and performing one last superbly childish gesture by picking up—that is, withdrawing—in the British open championship at St. Andrews.

I learned quite a bit at Hoylake, which was well dried out with the turf hard and the greens like glass; they don't water the greens over there; they believe in letting nature take its course, with golf. And I don't know but they're right. The Americans had a regular invasion organized and won the international match (an informal one) which presaged the Walker Cup competitions of these days, the latest of which our boys won after a terrific struggle at St. Andrews last year.

I played the quaintest golf all through Britain; good and bad and terrible golf. In my first match in the championship I played well and beat a chap named Manford with a card of about par. Then I met a Mr. Hamlet, who shot an 87—and I was just good enough to beat him 1 up. I had to win the last two holes to do it, and he assisted me ably by missing a four-foot putt at the seventeenth, while my uncertain putt at the last green, half-stymied by his previous stroke, hit his ball at the edge of the cup, and mine dropped in and his stayed out. That was plain luck.

Then I played a good round against Robert Harris and won, 6-5, and then a genial, sandy-haired gentleman, Allan Graham, fairly beat me to death with a queer brass putter. I lost 6-5, and Freddie Wright, my rival of the year before at the Engineers Club, was the last American, going out finally in the sixth round, to Bernard Darwin, the writer, I think.

And then the British open. . . . Five years later, the happiest evening of my golfing life was spent in an English taxicab trundling along through an English twilight, from St. Anne's-on-the-Sea to Liverpool, when I had been British open champion just two hours. It's something to win that old cup. . . .

This time, in 1921, I didn't win it, and what was immensely worse, I didn't play out the tournament. I have some sterling regrets in golf. This is the principal regret—that ever I quit in a competition. I know it's not regarded as reprehensible, in a medal-play competition against a field. I know some great players and fine sportsmen have done it, when they were simply going bad and had no chance for a good showing. But I was a youngster, still making my reputation. And I often have wished I could in some way offer a general apology for picking up my ball on the eleventh green of the third round, when I had a short putt left for a horrid 6. It means nothing to the world of golf. But it means something to me. Much more now than it did six years ago, when I took 46 for the first nine of the third round, and a 6 at the tenth and was making a 6 at the eleventh, and said to myself, "What's the use?"

Of course I continued to play, after tearing up my card—

that is a figurative term, by the way—and shot a very good 72 in the fourth round which would have put me in a decent position had I kept on in the competition. But my showing is not to be mentioned prominently in the same tournament where Jock Hutchison made that tremendous finish, and Roger Wethered, the English amateur, by stepping inadvertently on his own ball, lost a stroke and the championship, going into a tie with Jock, who beat him in the play-off.

Good old Jock Hutchison—I was playing with him when he made the eighth hole in one stroke, in the first round, and on the ninth, 306 yards, his drive rolled up to the hole, touched the rim, and switched off three inches away. He was that close to making two holes in succession in one stroke! Tommy Kerrigan was on the green when Jock drove, not expecting to reach it, and he said the ball really should have dropped; it was just like a putt that meets with hard luck.

I never shall forget Jock in that tournament. He was set like a piece of flint to win; and he shot miraculous golf, and then some terrible golf, and he came up to the last round, just as Wethered had finished, with a round of 70 to tie. And 70 at St. Andrews is—well, go out to your home course and shoot for yourself a 66. That will be about the idea. Especially if you can fancy the British open championship hanging on it.

Jock did just that; perhaps the greatest round of golf in the history of open championships. He did a 70, where par is a solemn 73 with only two par 3 holes in it. And he beat Roger in the play-off, and we went back to the United States to try our fortune in the American open, with Duncan and Mitchell in the field, at the Columbia Country Club, Washington.

The greens were essentially skittish, at Columbia, and of all the loose putting I ever committed, this was the time and the place. Also they had an 18-hole qualifying round—a palpable crime—and a lot of us nearly didn't qualify, I being one, with a 6 on the first hole which might have been anything, had I not got out of the woods.

I had a wild sort of first round, playing with Gene Sarazen, and finished with a 78, nine strokes back of Jim Barnes, who was on his way to victory. In the second round I got going and seemed likely to shoot almost anything, down to a silly 65. I exploded on the second nine, lost a hatful of strokes and still finished with a 71, five strokes back of Barnes. The third round I was shooting just as well up to the green. But, believe it or not, I used forty putts on the 18 holes, and with 37 other strokes, and putting for a birdie on every green but two, I had a rotten 77 and was out of it except for the craziest kind of a miracle. That was the worst putting round I ever had in a championship. The next worst was 39 putts in the fourth round of the British open at St. Anne's in 1926.

Well, when the final round started I was a matter of nine strokes back of Barnes and of course there was nothing to do but shoot the works. I started 3-3-4-3, two under par. On the long fifth I was set to get home in 2 and pick up another stroke. I pulled the second out of bounds. And I pulled the next one out of bounds. I took a 9 on that accursed hole and was through. I played as well as I could for a 77, and again Chick Evans, finishing in a 75, nosed me out by one stroke for the place of leading amateur. Barnes won with nine strokes to spare; a grand 289, with Freddie McLeod and Walter Hagen tied for second place at 298. Evans was fourth, 302, and I was fifth, 303, tied with Emmett French and Alex Smith. Alex and I were the oldest and the youngest players in the championship.

I had moved up from eighth to fifth, in the United States

open championship. But I didn't celebrate. . . . Walter Hagen said at Columbia I would win the open before I won the amateur championship. I thought he was kidding. But he was right.

CHAPTER EIGHT

ST. LOUIS—AND WHAT IS CHAMPIONSHIP?

THE remainder of the good year 1921 may be dismissed, first, with another lesson in the western open championship, where a stiff breeze blew me completely out of a fine start—I hadn't learned to play the wind then, not having had much of it at home, and the British experience being too short a period to teach me the lesson. I led the field at the end of two rounds in the western open at Oakwood, near Cleveland, and detonated completely in the third. With a card of 294, I finished in a tie for fourth place with Joe Kirkwood, while Walter Hagen went on to win handily.

But I got another lesson in 1921—the amateur championship at St. Louis, when we had a further flavor of international competition in the entry of Willie Hunter, who had won the British championship that same season at Hoylake, where Mr. Allan Graham so conclusively exterminated me in the fourth round. Willie came over to play in our national amateur championship at the St. Louis Country Club, and, gosh, how I pined for a chance to get at him! Now (thought I) we've got some regular greens that will hold a pitch and not skid a putt off into a bunker. Now (thought I) we've got some regular turf, and Willie can't run his drives a hundred yards or so after they hit the ground. Just let me at him, I reflected, more or less fatuously.

But most of all I wanted to win this championship. I was getting along. I'd been to Britain. I'd played in three national open championships and four national amateur championships. I was now a veteran, at the age of 19 years. It was time to win something that counted.

I started blithely enough, qualifying in 151 for the two rounds, seven strokes back of Francis Ouimet, who was medalist, and a dozen strokes ahead of the top score. I beat my first man, Clarence Wolff, 12-11, and my second, Dr. O. F. Willing, 9-8, and everybody, including myself, fancied I was set to kill off the British champion when I met him in Round 3.

All in all, I suspect I got more education out of that match than from any other I ever played. I could outdrive Hunter freely from the tee. And the rest of my game was working well enough to suit me. But he stuck to me like a bulldog. I was playing well in the morning round and was 2 up at the luncheon intermission. I found myself saying (to myself), "Only 2 up!" I worried a trifle about that, and changed my pants for luck, donning a pair of long flannel trousers with a pin-stripe. I was beginning to think a little about my sartorial appearance on the golf course, and I liked those pants and also fancied they were lucky, since I had won a couple of matches in them.

Willie picked up a hole at the third in the afternoon. We battled on to the eighth tee and I had got the hole back and was still 2 up, with eleven to play.

The eighth at St. Louis is called the Cape Hole, and it is a dog-leg to the right, giving you a fair pitch after a straight drive out the fairway. If you want to carry the tall trees in the angle you may get much nearer the green, even on the front of it, if you are bold and have sufficient *gluteus maximus* in your stroke. I decided to carry the trees—indeed, I had been doing that all week—and pick up another hole (possibly) and break Willie's obstinate back right there.

I went for the carry over the angle, and the ball, for the first time all week, caught the topmost branch of the tallest tree, and dropped in a ditch full of stones and weeds, with at least one rabbit in it—he came bouncing out as my first blast failed to extract the ball.

Willie won that hole with a par 4. He won the next hole, a par 5, while I was still reflecting on the mutability of fortune. I went 1 up at the long thirteenth; he sank a thirty-foot putt to square at the fourteenth. I blew the fifteenth on a short putt after a convenient spectator had saved me from going out of bounds, and he sank a long putt again to go 2 up at the Redan Hole. I had a five-yard putt for a win at the next hole, the thirty-fifth of the match, to stay in it, but I missed, and we shook hands.

That night O. B. Keeler, who is working with me on these memoirs, came to my room at the hotel—rather, I was in his room, waiting for him, Dad having gone to sleep, most unhappy.

He told me I had lost the match, and very likely the championship, on the eighth hole in the afternoon round, when, with Hunter 2 down, I had taken the chance instead of making him take the chance.

I told him he might be right but I could not play match golf that way. I had to play every stroke for all there was in it. I could not play safe. He said that was a laudable frame of mind, but it would cost me a lot of tournaments. And still I don't know. It is true that since I started playing match golf as near as I can like medal golf—shooting for par and letting my opponent shoot what he can—I have managed to win a couple of match-play national championships. And three open, or medal-play, championships. Old Man Par after all is the toughest opponent you can have, and if you play him and play him close he generally will look out for the other fellow. But there's that old maxim: "When you get him 1 doon, get him 2 doon; when you get him 3 doon, get him 4 doon!" I sort of like that, too. Even if it did kill me off, against Willie Hunter, at St. Louis.

St. Louis, too, marked the next to the last battle involving calories. I continued to eat a lot of food at St. Louis, and insisted on ice-cream, or (as a compromise) loganberry ice. And my afternoon rounds were not so good. O. B. was arguing with me a good deal about that. After Skokie, in the open championship next year, we began to get together. And now it's toast and tea, between rounds; nothing more.

But for a terrific rain that drenched the St. Louis Country Club course, I think to this day that Willie Hunter would have had a great chance to win. The rain came along after he had licked me, and against Bob Gardner, with his long-carrying shots. Willie was at a disadvantage. Bob beat him 6-5 and went on to meet Jesse Guilford, the Boston Siege Gun—the

Great Excavator—in the finals, played on a soaked course and partly in the rain.

They were not far apart in the morning and up to the sixth hole of the afternoon round, and then Big Jess cut loose a blast of golf that makes anything else I have seen in the amateur championship look rather pallid. Beginning with the sixth hole, par is 4-3-4-5 through No. 9. Jesse traveled 3-2-3-4, four birdies in a row; four strokes under par. And that finished the gallant Bob, who never quit trying, but lost at the thirtieth green, 7-6.

I went away from St. Louis with a curious ache in my chest and a definite ache in my left leg, which was suffering from several patches of varicose veins. . . . The first ache I could not define well. More and more I felt a load on me, going into these devilish championships. I always wanted to win, and hoped I might win; but now I felt more and more I was expected to win. I read the papers and once in a while I heard the golf writers talking, and talked with them, about the championships. And more and more they kept saying that I was as good a golfer as anybody else; perhaps the best shotmaker among the amateurs; and that I really ought to step out and win. It was getting on my nerves, and I didn't know why or what it was, this curious responsibility. I hadn't asked for it. I was just a boy playing golf. And now in a gradual but apparently universal sort of way, I was being expected to win a national championship. I was expected to win—not just to shoot a fancy round here and there, or beat some classic opponent. I was expected to win a championship. . . . It was at St. Louis I overheard a golf writer say to another, after Willie Hunter had stopped me: "Sure—he's the greatest shotmaker we have. But he can't win."

Championship. . . . Championship. I thought it over, in a

Bobby Jones relaxing in his usual golfing attire, circa 1925.

A typical Bobby grin.

kid's way. Not beating a great player now and then. Not winning a medal round, here and there. Not drubbing the boys back home in a state or a sectional tournament. . . . Championship—championship. Seventy-two holes of medal play in the national open, or beating five men, in succession, in the national amateur. So that's it. No matter how prettily you play your shots. No matter how well you swing or how sweetly the ball behaves—after all, it's only championship that counts, the way most of us have come to look at it.

Please don't understand me as being unappreciative of my good fortune in the matter of championship. But that is part of what I mean. There was so much of fortune, so much of luck, in my winning that I now feel more than ever that the popular value of championship is a factitious rating; and that golf is too great and too fine a game, and too much an epitome of life itself, for such a ranking to do it justice. . . . I can speak frankly about this, now that I have won some spurs. I can say with all my heart that it means a great deal to me, for my name to be on three of the four major golfing trophies of the world. And I can also say with all my heart that I think it's a rotten shame for us so readily to overlook the fine fellows and the truly great golfers who for one reason or another never have got within that charmed circle of national championship. . . . I think they do not overlook them so readily in Britain as we do; I think we are more enamored of championship over here. And they have the better view, it seems to me. It appears a poor thing that the late Jack Graham should be ranked an inferior golfer to some of us champions, simply because he lacked the plain brute endurance to play through a long, gruelling tournament. A strong back and a weak mind and a lot of this stuff they call the will to win—another name for stupid persistence, frequently—have made many a golfing champion who hadn't the shots or the heart or the character of Jack Graham, and a lot more I could name, who never got into the newspaper headlines. . . . The road to championship was a hard one, for me, and it took seven years in the climbing. And when I got there, at Inwood, my first feeling was that nothing mattered—I had broken through. And next, when I missed some of the elation I had expected, I just said to myself: "You lucky dog!" I think no golfer ever properly appreciates the amount of luck needed to win a championship until he has been on the inside and has won one.

Funny thing—all through this little story I've felt more impelled to write about tournaments that I lost than those which I won. The championships I won seemed sort of inevitable; I hadn't so much to do with them. But the championships I lost. . . . There was a lot of fighting, and fighting by myself. We are coming to a couple now; the national open at Skokie, near Chicago, and the national amateur, at Brookline, near Boston, in 1922. I was only a stroke behind Sarazen at Skokie, and the seventeenth hole of the final round broke me, as it broke grand old John Black, with whom I was tied for second place.

I started the season of 1922 with an operation, or rather four operations, on my left leg for the swollen veins which had troubled me the previous year, and was out of the hospital less than two weeks when the southern amateur championship was played at East Lake, my home course. I had played just nine holes, and had put in perhaps half an hour on a practice tee, hitting iron shots, when I went into it, my leg still in bandages.

This tournament probably was the best-scoring prolonged event I ever played. The course was 6700 yards around with a par of 72. I qualified modestly in a triple-tie with Perry Adair, my old partner, and Tub Palmer of Miami, with a score of 75. Counting this and all subsequent rounds in the five matches, my score was ten strokes better than par at the conclusion. I won the tournament, got my name on the great George W. Adair memorial trophy, and have not played in a southern championship since. Perry won it next year at Roebuck, Birmingham, so our names are together on the cup that commemorates his father, a great sportsman and the man who, I think, did more for golf in Atlanta and the South than any other.

The Skokie course was pretty easy, I fancied, and I came on my game about right, shooting 74-72-70 in the first three rounds. I remember I felt sure I could do a 68 in the last round, to bring the score down symmetrically, and as I was tied for the lead with Bill Mehlhorn after three rounds, I felt this ought to be good enough. If Bill could do better, why, all right. Walter Hagen had jumped into the lead with a 68 in the first round. I was playing with him and was six strokes back, but Walter found all the traps on the course in the next nine holes and I caught up with him.

I felt I might win when I started the last round. Gene Sarazen started an hour and a half ahead of me (I was playing with George Duncan) and as Gene was four strokes back of the lead nobody fancied he had a chance. But he spun off one of those great rounds of his and as I went to the tenth tee he holed out on the last green, and the word was flashed about that he had done a 68.

It was a stiff jolt, as I wasn't going well enough to keep faith with the 68 I had wanted for my own fourth round; indeed, I was out in 36 and now had to do another 36 to tie Gene.

Here's where the iron certitude of medal competition bears

down on you. You *know* what you have to do, in that last round. It is not one man whom you can see, and who may make a mistake at any moment, with whom you are battling. It is an iron score, something already in the book. So many holes—so many strokes. I've tried it both ways, setting the pace and trying to come up from behind. And I don't know which is harder. But either is harder, for me, than match play, though everybody fancies the opposite, because I have been rather more successful at medal play.

Well, I missed a putt at the tenth hole and lost one of my strokes. I had to pick it up somewhere on par, and instead I lost another, pitching over the green at the twelfth. I was working as hard as I ever did in my life, and when I sank a thirty-five foot putt for a birdie 3 at the fourteenth I found myself flat on the turf as the ball dropped. . . . I was unconsciously putting what they call body-English on the ball, trying to pull it into the hole.

I had one stroke back and felt I could pick up the other at the finishing hole, a par 5 of nearly 500 yards, which I could reach with two good bangs. I just missed another birdie at the fifteenth, got my par 4 at the sixteenth, and fired a long drive over a towering bunker at the left of the fairway on the seventeenth, taking the straight line to the green. Here came the break. A par 4 here and a birdie 4 at the last hole would tie for the lead with Gene. My drive had cut off a lot of distance and left me an easy iron shot to the big green. But the ball had taken a curious kick to the left and was lying badly in a roadway, under a tree. . . . I had to hack it out in the hope that it would run up the sloping green. It just reached the front edge and rolled back. I failed to chip close and missed the putt, taking a 5. . . . Well, I tried so hard for an eagle 3 on the long eighteenth that my second shot was pulled off the back edge of the green, but I pitched up and got down a good putt for the birdie 4 and a tie with John Black, who, with a better chance than I in the last nine, also had been ruined by the seventeenth hole, which cost him a 6.

It was on the way home to Atlanta after Skokie that O. B. asked me, consolingly, what I'd do if I played as poor a game as he did. I told him I'd have a lot more fun out of it. And I meant it. This championship quest was getting more than a bit thick.

I was moving up, slowly, in the national open. In 1920 I finished in eighth place. In 1921 it was fifth place. And here I was in second place. But there is a lot of difference between second place and championship—also between a tie for first place and championship, as I was to find out in 1925. This devilish championship—a single stroke, and one man is open champion, and two others are merely runners-up. I felt sort of tired and old, going back to Atlanta. It was a hard thing to buck. In every open championship there would be three hundred or more entered, and upwards of a hundred qualified. And of them, one, or maybe two or three or half a dozen, would be shooting at top form. And there was only one of me, and if I wasn't at top form I'd be out of luck, and if I should be at top form, why, there were the others also at top form; and the breaks would settle it. It sounds like a conceited thing to say, but I've never played really hot golf in a national open championship yet, and I've played in ten, counting one Canadian and two British. That makes forty rounds, and I've never shot under 70 yet in a single round. Most of the other boys have. I wonder if I ever will.

We will resume with the national amateur at Brookline in 1922, where I got my tidiest licking, from Jess Sweetser.

CHAPTER NINE

BREAKING THROUGH

I WAS 20 years old, and had been graduated as a mechanical engineer from the Georgia School of Technology, when I started north in August, 1922, to play in the first international golf match for the Walker Cup, at the National Links, Southampton, L. I., and then in the national amateur championship at Brookline, just out of Boston. I remember I was boning away at Cicero's Orations Against Cataline, on the train; trying to catch up on some Latin work in order to enter Harvard in quest of a B.S. degree. I remember also envying Cicero because he evidently thought so well of himself. If I only thought as much of my golfing ability (I considered) as Cicero thought of his statesmanship, I might do better in these blamed tournaments. You know, Cicero was a long way from hating himself.

The American team won the Walker Cup match at the National Links rather handily. My singles match was against Roger Wethered and we had a fine battle in which my putting saved me until he began pulling his tremendous drives to the impossible rough, when I managed to beat him. Jess Sweetser and I were partnered in the foursomes and we won our match, too, against "Chubby" Hooman and Willie Torrance. The next time we played together Jess did most of the playing.

This was a few days later at Brookline. The first qualifying day was beautiful and the next was as wet a day as I ever saw connected with a golf tournament. Some remarkable play ensued. Chick Evans, playing every hole of the eighteen in a drenching rain, turned in a 74. I had scored a 73 on the fine day, and was quite proud of a 72 played mostly in a hard rain, but Jesse Guilford, with a 74 in the previous round came in with a 70 in the rain and with a total of 144 was the medalist. I was second with 145. Sweetser played only ordinarily well, for him, with 152, being comfortably qualified, ten strokes below the top score.

Jess at once started winning his matches by wide margins—10-9, and then 7-6—beating Willie Hunter, who had defeated me the previous year at St. Louis—and then stopping Guilford 4-3. Evans after a close match with John Anderson also was winning comfortably. I was having close and hard battles, two of them with players I never had heard of before—James J. Beadle and William McPhail—while in the second round I had my usual struggle with Bob Gardner, much of it in the rain, and was fortunate enough to win. Rudy Knepper was performing spectacularly, defeating two British entrants, Torrance and Cyril Tolley, and Francis Ouimet. He evidently shot himself pretty well out, and Chick Evans, who was playing fine golf, beat him 11-9 in the semi-final round. While this was going on Sweetser and I came together and at the second hole of the 36-hole match I got a jolt on the button which after nearly five years still makes me groggy when I recall it.

We halved the first hole rather sloppily. The second is a drive and pitch up a hill, and I was slightly in front from the tee. Jess was about 90 yards from the green and used that devilishly accurate spade which has dug the grave for so many golfers. He hit the ball firmly and crisply and we saw it land on the green. Then there was a great roar from the gallery, which had gone ahead and was ringed about the green. . . . Jess had holed an eagle 2! . . . . Well, I still had a shot for a half, and I played it the best I could. And we heard another roar from the gallery. But my ball was still up. . . . It was six inches from the hole. My birdie 3 wasn't good enough for a half.

Sometimes I think that punch settled it. I don't in the least mind saying it jarred me. For nine holes I played rather poor golf, and also met with a bit of bad luck when my ball, pitched well on to the sixth green, picked up a chunk of sticky black soil and I never did get it into the hole; it was like putting an egg. Jess was trapped with his second and won the hole easily. I was 6 down at the turn.

But Jess was shooting grand golf. In that round he lowered a course record which had stood for thirteen years. And while I got my game together and shot the second nine in 34, I only picked up one hole on him, the seventeenth, where he made his only mistake. Five down starting the afternoon round, I had to go for everything, of course, and Jess, playing steadily, added to his lead at every mistake I made and chopped my head off, 8-7, at the long eleventh hole. . . . I remember thinking it was adding insult to injury, beating me at the most distant point from the club house, so I would have to haul my bedraggled self nearly a mile before I could sit down and rest.

In that tournament I suppose Sweetser shot the most devastating golf ever seen in our national amateur. Anyway, he beat Willie Hunter, Jesse Guilford, me, and Chick Evans in succession, and all of us were rated tough customers. . . . I'll never forget the shot that really closed Chick out, though the finish was at the thirty-fourth green, 3-2. Chick was making a hard fight, and though he was 3 down at the fourteenth tee after messing up the short thirteenth, he looked like getting one back when he planted a great iron second shot six feet from the pin. But Sweetser stuck an iron shot a foot closer; Chick missed his putt, and Jess sank his for a birdie 3, and that virtually settled the match.

So that was 1922, when I was 20 years old, and I had now played in eleven national championships, amateur and open, and still was outside. The thorn was beginning to rankle in earnest. Even the kindly thing Jess Sweetser said, when I congratulated him again after he had won the championship, hurt me a good deal as I thought of it later. "Thank you, Bobby," he said. "I beat the best man in the field yesterday." He meant me. And it was a pretty thing to say. But there was that increasing insistence—a great golfer, but it's time he won something; a great golfer, but he can't win! I was now wondering what was the matter. If I was really a great golfer—what was the matter? Or was I a great golfer? I could hit the shots well; I couldn't help knowing that. But was I a golfer, or only one of those hapless mechanical excellencies known as a great shot-maker, who cannot connect the great shots in sufficient numbers to win anything?

I was beginning to brood about it a good deal. And I knew

Dad was hurt by my licking at Brookline. . . . Dear old boy! He went to one more amateur championship, at Flossmoor, and saw me take another licking. And then he decided he was jinxing me, and he has never been to one since. He went to the national open at Columbus last year—and up to the last few holes he thought he had jinxed me again. He's taken a lot more punishment than I have, I guess.

Back home again, I was out at East Lake one Saturday afternoon playing with Dad and Tess Bradshaw and Forrest Adair, Jr.—it was the sixteenth of September, the next Saturday after Brookline—when I got going and shot the lowest-scoring round of my life, though not the best played. The course is 6700 yards around and par is 72 and I had a card of 63, with all putts holed. I had nine pars and nine birdies. As I recall it, this was the card:

Par (out). . . .	434	553	435 — 36		
Me.	324	443	434 — 31		
Par (in).	434	455	443 — 36	——	72
Me.	433	454	333 — 32	——	63

But what of it? I heard a lot about that round, and there were stories about it in the papers. And every time I saw another reference to it, or somebody mentioned it to me, I'd think, why couldn't I have matched a round something like that with Jess Sweetser's 69 at Brookline, or Gene Sarazen's 68 in the last round of the national open at Skokie. . . . I was getting a sort of championship complex, I suppose. Instead of regarding my game as a pleasant diversion and a fine sport, I was thinking of it continually as a possible means to championship; not so much because I wanted to be a champion as because everybody seemed to have concluded I ought to be one. Every tournament I entered I was selected as one of the favorites. And more and more it was getting on my nerves. At times I could almost laugh at the situation—to myself—when I reflected on what right I had, in the face of this almost universal demand, to refuse to be a champion? . . . . That is why the open tournament at Inwood the next year was the hardest of all. Sometimes I think that if either of two particular shots there had failed to come off, I never would have won a championship. . . . Certainly not that one. But that was a sort of crisis. If the long lane had not turned at Inwood, I think sometimes it would have gone straight on to its end in the shadows.

I went to Harvard that fall and was busy there and happy, and played next to no golf at all until the following early summer when I came home and began trying to get ready for the open championship at Inwood, Long Island. I couldn't get going and Stewart Maiden said he had better accompany me to the tournament, which he did. My first practice rounds at Inwood were terrible. It's a great course, and narrow, and severe on anything like wild play. I was continually in trouble from the tee, in practice, and it was hard to get under 80. I was fearfully depressed. The full heft of responsibility seems to have hit me, at Inwood—the idea of being a great golfer (as people kept saying) who couldn't win. It was at Inwood I gave over anything like an explanation to myself, when I had finished the fourth round with a rotten 6 on the last hole. . . . I'll tell you about that.

In some way, when the tournament started and the strain came on, I got the shots working pretty well and had a 71 in the first round, which was a stroke under par, and a stroke back of Jock Hutchison, whose 70 was the best round of the tournament. I was pleased with the morning round and satisfied with the afternoon round, which was 73, also a stroke back of Jock, who had a great 142 for the day. I was 144. Bobby Cruickshank had come in with a fine 72 in the afternoon and was third with 145. Only three other scores were under 150. As I say, it was a tough course.

As I now learned, the third round in an open championship is a great one for blowing up, and if you find yourself going a bit sourly under the pressure, the thing to do is to stick to your business and save all the strokes you can. I went bad in the third round and when I finished with a 76 I was surprised to find I was out in front by three strokes. Cruickshank took a 78 and Hutchison, who had led both of us the first day, had collapsed about midway of the round and finished with an 82. After 54 holes I stood 220; Cruickshank 223; and the Hutch 224.

It was then I learned what a devilish thing it is to be setting the pace. At the luncheon intermission I figured that another 73 would win for me, or even a 74, and probably a 75. And I made the fatal mistake of playing for a certain figure that was *not* Old Man Par. What I should have done, of course, was to set my sights on par and shoot for that as best I could and shut out of my mind Bobby Cruickshank and Jock Hutchison and the rest of them. I admit I was thinking about Bobby Cruickshank, who was starting behind me. I heard that he was the only one with a real chance to catch me.

I started badly and was out in 39, two strokes over par. But I had never been over 35 coming in, and I wasn't much worried. When I holed a six-yard putt for a birdie 3 on the tenth, and after par on the next three holes got a birdie 4 on the long fourteenth, I felt I was safe. I had a bit of luck getting a par 3 on the tricky fifteenth, and then, on three holes of 4-4-4, on which I had not used more than twelve strokes in any previous round, I finished feebly with 5-5-6, chucking away four strokes to par, and coming as near as possible to chucking away my chance for the championship.

The strain of setting the pace simply got me, I suppose. You have to figure on that, as on any other hazard. I pulled my second shot out of bounds at the fifteenth and was lucky to get a 5 with a six-foot putt after a mound had kicked my next attempt on to the green near the hole. I missed the seventeenth green with a long pitch and took another 5. And at the last hole of the long grind I played too carefully, taking a spoon against the breeze for my second shot over the lagoon, and pulling the ball off to the left, back of a pot-bunker. . . . It also was under a chain about the twelfth tee, which the officials removed, while I sat on the turf five minutes and brooded over my rotten play. After which I got up and popped the ball neatly into the bunker, and finished with a horrid 6.

I must have looked pretty bad when I walked off the green because when O. B. came up to shake hands with me I could see him blink before he said:

"Bob, I think you're champion. Cruickshank will never catch you."

Then I said what was in my heart and had been there longer than I like to admit:

"Well, I didn't finish like a champion. I finished like a yellow dog."

And I went up to my room at the club to wait for the jury to come in, Bobby Cruickshank being the jury.

Cruickshank did catch me. He came to the last hole, after some troubles of his own, and a bad 6 on the sixteenth, with a birdie 3 to tie the count. And he made it—one of the greatest holes ever played in golf. It was far and away the greatest, for me. It gave me a chance to get square with myself. If Bobby Cruickshank also had bogged down at the finish, and I had been left out in front, I'd never have felt I had won that championship. I'd have felt that Cruickshank lost it. Because I knew that, whatever else anyone might do or fail to do, I had finished four strokes down to Old Man Par on the last three holes; I had finished like a yellow dog.

It was never a matter between Cruickshank and me, that last round, though I made the mistake of thinking about him. It was a matter between Old Man Par and me. And I was level with Old Man Par with three holes to play; and if I'd only stepped with him—well, there wouldn't have been any play-off.

Anyway, that gave me the chance to see if I really was hopelessly weak under the belt; and I heard later that the betting was 10 to 7 on Cruickshank to beat me in the play-off, because he had the moral advantage of coming from behind. . . . I felt all right as we started, only sort of numb. And we had a curious round of medal play. Of the eighteen holes we halved only three. I was par for the first six and was 2 strokes behind. Cruickshank was playing wonderfully. He drove first at No. 7, a tough one-shotter of 223 yards with out-of-bounds (a two-stroke penalty) on each side of a narrow lane-like fairway. Cruickshank played safe, an iron, short of the green. I had to decide between a safe shot with an iron, like his, or going for the green with a spoon in the effort to pick up a stroke—and with the excellent chance of going out of bounds on one side or the other, which would mean blowing the championship then and there. . . . Much has been written about my iron shot on the finishing hole, which is credited with the title. But it was nothing compared to this one, in strain. For I was still conscious at the seventh. I do not remember anything about that iron shot on the eighteenth hole, except suddenly seeing the ball on this green, near the pin. . . . Here I had to decide. . . . I took the spoon, and I got the ball on the green. Bobby failed to chip dead, missed a ten-foot putt, and I picked up a stroke. He missed another ten-footer to get it back on the next hole, and missed a five-footer at the ninth, and we were square.

Then we collapsed at the short tenth, with a 5 and a 6, and I was ahead. Two bad 5's halved the next and I pitched two feet from the pin at the short twelfth and had two strokes in hand, only to lose them when Bobby nearly sank an eagle 3 at the 500-yard fourteenth, and I messed up the par 3 fifteenth for a terrible 5, while he took a 4. I got a stroke at the sixteenth and he got it back at the seventeenth and we were square with one to play.

The strain had killed us off; anyway it had killed me. Bobby pulled his drive to a road back of a tree and could not go for the green with his second, playing a fine iron short of the perilous water in front of the green. I sliced to the short rough and the ball lay on hard ground, clean. . . . I suppose I had to decide again whether to play safe or go for it with an iron of about 200 yards. But I don't remember it. Stewart Maiden was near me. He told me later I never played a shot more promptly or decisively. He says I picked a No. 2 iron from the bag and banged it. . . . I saw the ball on the green near the pin. Next thing I knew somebody was propping me up by the arm. . . . I won the hole with a 4 to Bobby's 6. And the championship. . . . The first conscious thought I had was: "I don't care what happens now." I had won a championship.

CHAPTER TEN

AFTER SEVEN LEAN YEARS

I DON'T just know how to go on writing about the tournaments after the United States open championship at Inwood in 1923, when I managed to get out of the seven lean years and win my first major title. You see, in the seven years previous I had played in eleven national championships and had not won any of them. I broke through at Inwood, and since then things somehow have been different. It's an odd thing to say, but I can't find near as much to write about the last ten championships in which I played as the first eleven. Yet I didn't win any of the first eleven, and, one way or another, I won five of the next ten; five in four years. Something has been different, since Inwood. . . . I remember when I went to Chicago later in 1923, for the national amateur championship at Flossmoor, all the critics said I was virtually sure to win; I had a title under my belt, now; I had tasted blood—that sort of thing. Whereupon Max Marston put me out in the second round, my promptest exit from a national amateur. I was pretty well disgusted but not hurt as I was at Brookline. I'd won a championship, anyway. I remember telling O. B. that night at the hotel that I was going on playing in the amateur championships, if I never won one.

"I was beaten in the second round here," I said, "and I've now been beaten in every round except the first, and I'm going to play at Merion next year and probably I'll lose in the first round there."

He said:

"Yes—and you've won in every round except the *last*. Maybe it will be that one, at Merion."

Well, it turned out that way. But we haven't got there yet. In 1923 I topped off my win at Inwood by losing to Max Marston at Flossmoor, and let me say that Max earned that victory, which he followed by going on to defeat Sweetser on the thirty-eighth green of the final round, winning the championship. I shot some hot golf at Max, setting a new course record in the morning round and being 2 up on him. But in the last nineteen holes of that match, from the seventeenth to the thirty-fifth inclusive, Max was 5 strokes under par, so you see I was not handing him anything. I decided then, as I told O. B., I was never going to win an amateur championship. Somebody always went crazy against me.

But I carried away a crumb of comfort from Flossmoor, and a valuable lesson in tournament golf. Chick Evans and I were tied at 149 for the 36 holes of medal play—par at Flossmoor was 74—and as both of us were erased early in the match play we got together to settle the medal in a play-off the day after

Marston had beaten me. I set a new medal course record with a 72 and won the round, Chick having a 76. . . . Then I got to wondering why the devil I didn't play that way, in matches. And that was the lesson I learned. That was the answer, for me. If only I could manage to shoot against Old Man Par in the matches, as I did in the medal play events, and (to be impolite) let my opponents go to the devil, why, maybe I either wouldn't run into so many hot rounds, or, when I did run into them, I wouldn't be so much affected. I thought I'd give it a try anyway. . . . It worked pretty well. Since that licking at Flossmoor I have played in exactly twenty matches in four national amateur championships. I've won eighteen and lost two. And the two I lost were to Andrew Jamieson, in the sixth round of the British championship at Muirfield, and George Von Elm, in the fifth (and final) round of the United States amateur at Baltusrol. And Jamieson was two under par for the duration of the match, with never a hole above par; and George was a stroke under par for the 35 holes we played. So I've certainly no complaint to make in either case, especially as I was a couple of strokes above par against Jamieson, and a stroke over par against George.

Here's the idea, as I see it. The general opinion is that I am a better medal player than match player; but I don't see much difference, except that I've been a bit more successful at medal play and have a better-looking record there. The cards will show that I play about the same, match and medal. It has been my fortune to encounter some very admirable golf in my match play ventures, good enough to stop me in 18 or 36 holes, while my own play was sufficiently good to have kept me well in the running had the competition been extended to 72 holes, as in the medal events. My two rounds against Marston at Flossmoor, or my two rounds against Von Elm at

Baltusrol, while not good enough to win in either case, would have been eminently satisfactory for two rounds in an open championship, with two more to follow. Either pair of rounds would have been better than my first 36 holes in the last United States open championship at Columbus, when I was 6 strokes back of the leader, and still managed to scrape out a victory in the next 36 holes. . . . I suppose I am rather a better medal player, after all. It's a different feeling. In match play I rarely can get away from the notion that each hole is a detached and separate bout; you may take ten strokes on one hole but that's merely one hole gone, and a 3 at the next may get it back. But if you take ten strokes on one hole in a medal event—goodbye, championship! So in medal play I feel that I'm at work on a big, definite structure; adding this par hole to another par hole, as one story is added to another, on a tall building; and that if I blow a short putt here, why, I'll get down a long one later on. Saving the strokes—that was the answer, for me. I don't play any better golf than I did five or six years ago. The pleasant things that have been written about my getting control of my temper, with better play resulting, are all bunk; I get just as mad as I ever did, missing a simple shot. I don't throw my club away now; that's all. I don't hit the shots any better, and I don't pitch nearly so well as I used to, in the days before I broke through.

But what I have managed to do—the little thing that has done most to win those five major championships in four years—is simply to save that one little stroke a round that used to get away from me, through carelessness or dumb play. I fancy it's really less than a stroke a round. Gauged by the open championships—four rounds of medal play—it's only two or three strokes in the four rounds; a half or three-fourths of a stroke a round.

I can supply a good illustration of how strokes can be wasted, and paradoxically enough the illustration is taken from a championship I won: the national open at Columbus in July, 1926—a bit of honest confession that I still chuck strokes away through petulance or carelessness or dumb play.

It was at the end of the worst round I ever shot in a national open championship. Everything had gone wrong. I was not playing well, and things were breaking badly to boot. I had incurred a penalty stroke at the tenth hole, the ball lying against a stone wall which was ruled to be part of a water hazard. Then, after making something of a rally, I still had the prospect of a 74 to put with my opening round of 70, which wouldn't have been so bad, and would certainly have kept me up with the leaders.

Then I got to the fifteenth green, and when I grounded my putter in front of the ball, squaring the blade to the line, the darned ball rolled—it had been held up on a slope of the green by the stiff wind, and when I cut off the breeze it moved about an inch. Well, there was another penalty stroke, and it looked as if I were being picked on. Still I had a chance for a 75. And then I took three putts at the seventeenth. . . . Well, I was tired and stale and sick and mad clear through. And now I had to get a birdie 4 on the 480-yard home hole for a card of 76.

I walloped the drive as hard as I could; harder than I could, for my timing was slow and the ball was shoved to the right in the deep rough, which was like hay, at Columbus. There was a big bunker 150 yards ahead, up the fairway, and I should have taken a mashie or a spade and made sure of a par 5 by hewing the ball out onto the fairway short of the bunker, an easy pitch from the green. But no—I was mad, and I took a No. 2 iron and decided to bang that ball over the bunker, near enough to the green for a wee pitch and the chance at a

Robert T. Jones, Jr., with his father,
Colonel Robert P. Jones, in 1924.

Bobby poses with Jess Sweetser, Gene Sarazen and Walter Hagen in 1926 after returning from Great Britain.

birdie 4. So I slugged with the iron in the deep rough and the ball went about twenty yards, and remained in the hay. That settled it. I didn't even change clubs. I scarcely took a stance for the next shot, and pulled the ball clear across the fairway into the rough on the other side, failed to reach the green with my pitch, chipped five feet from the pin—and missed the putt. I took a 7 on that wretched hole, and a 79 for the round; the worst round I ever shot in an American open championship. I was six strokes behind the leader, and that seemed to be plenty. And two of those strokes had been simply wasted; chucked away by dumb, petulant play. . . . At the last nine holes of that tournament next day I was four strokes back of Joe Turnesa and those wasted shots were bearing down furiously. I won out by a single stroke—that close to chucking away the chance to win the British and the American open championships in the same year.

Old Man Par, the imperturbable economist! Make a friend and a constant foe of him, and the other boys won't be so rough on you. They say I'm not so good a match player because I don't get many birdies. But I'll string along with Old Man Par if he'll only let me. I've never been in an open championship yet where par wasn't good enough to win; and only a few matches. Old Man Par—he never gets down in one putt, and he never takes three. I only wish I could be sure of shooting along with him, the next time I start!

This is getting away from Flossmoor rather too fast, the next stop being Oakland Hills, Detroit, for the national open, where I managed a finish that consoled me somewhat for bogging down so shamefully at Inwood. I made a birdie 4 on the very last hole, a matter of 475 yards against a hard wind, to go one stroke ahead of Bill Mehlhorn, who had finished with 301 and was leading the field. And then along came Cyril Walker with a great round in the wind and beat me by three strokes. I was runner-up again. . . . And I went to Merion, where I had started my national tournament career eight years before, rather curious to see who would beat me this time in the national amateur, and in what round. Also, I was going to try out the medal-play system in matches, if I could.

It worked pretty well. Not one of the boys went crazy against me, and I wasn't pressed hard after the second round, where Ducky Corkran gave me a grand scare after I had him dormie 5. Playing against Old Man Par kept me from worrying so much when Rudy Knepper started our afternoon round with a flock of birdies. And it saved me, with Francis Ouimet. . . . I simply couldn't play against Francis, so I concentrated on playing against Old Man Par, and the match ended on the twenty-sixth green, where my break against Bob Gardner had begun, eight years before. Of course I don't mean I shot precisely par all through that tournament. But I was able to play the old boy pretty close and it was good enough.

So I had won an amateur championship, too. And still I had shot just about the regular old brand of golf, it seemed. I remember a rude sort of thought, standing on the practice green before the club house, waiting for the cup presentation. I thought:

"Now I've won the blamed thing. And I didn't do anything, either!"

I meant, I hadn't done any more than I'd been doing. This time none of the boys went crazy against me. . . . Or at Oakmont, near Pittsburgh, in the next amateur championship, of 1925. Nobody shot a round under par at me, and only Watts Gunn, my own *protégé* from Atlanta, started to do it. Watts was the sensation of that championship, by all odds. He came up there unknown, to his first great tournament.

Against his first opponent, Vincent Bradford, he was 3 down through the eleventh hole and then started a winning run never equalled in any major tournament match—he won the next fifteen holes in succession and beat his man 11-10 at the twenty-sixth green. He then continued a string of fifty consecutive holes on the great Oakmont course in par, incidentally defeating Jess Sweetser 10-9, the worst beating Jess ever got; worse even than the one Jess had given me at Brookline three years before. And Watts and I came together in the finals; club-mates and warm friends—master and pupil, they called us—and before we reached the turn of the first round I was wondering why I had begged Watts' father to send him to Oakmont.

Briefly, I was a stroke better than par as I stood on the twelfth tee, and I was 1 down. Watts was shooting the hottest inspirational golf I had ever faced; I doubt if anybody ever saw much better; I was going at top speed; and the huge gallery was dizzy. So, incidentally, was I.

And this No. 12, remember, was the Ghost Hole, where the megaphone blast had struck me six years ago in the match with Davy Herron. . . . The writers called it the Ghost Hole, and speculated if its haunting memories would break my nerve in some crisis of 1925. . . . As suggested more than once before, the destiny of golf seems to play no favorites in the long run—if the run is long enough. After six years I was back at Oakmont, facing the Ghost Hole again. And this time my own *protégé* had me down and was playing like a man in a trance. And my third shot (the hole is of 600 yards) was bunkered at the green, and Watts' was well on, for a sure par 5. When I went down into that bunker I was morally certain of one thing. If Watts took that hole from me I'd never catch him. He was playing the most ferocious brand of inspirational golf I had ever seen; he was 2 under par now, and he was about to take another hole from me.

Well, destiny was on my side. That is all. The writers said afterward—some of them—that I had the match in hand all the way and kept the pressure on till the kid cracked. I say that if I had not managed to blast that ball out fairly well and get down a ten-foot putt for a half, the Ghost Hole would have done for me again.

As it was, I got the half in par 5, and was thereby inspired to start a hot run. I shot the remaining six holes of the round 3-3-4-3-3-4, finished the round 2 under par and 4 up on Watts, and started the afternoon round 4-3, which settled matters. . . . But I'll always believe the match turned on that ten-foot putt at the Ghost Hole.

Oddly enough, while my new system was meeting with almost startling success in the amateur championships, it was leaving me runner-up in the national open at Worcester, Mass., in 1925, as well as at Oakland Hills the previous year. I had a great battle with Old Man Par and Willie Macfarlane at Worcester, earlier in the summer, and lost to both of them. That was a tough one to lose. I started with a horrid 77 and was in thirty-sixth place, and at least one newspaper counted me out of it. I shot a 70 that afternoon and moved up to tenth position. Another 70 next morning—I never have broken 70 in a national open—put me in fourth place. And in the last round, with everybody blowing up, as usual, I managed to get a 74 and tie for first place with Willie Macfarlane, the tall and bespectacled Tuckahoe professional.

After pulling up that far I wanted awfully to win. Willie played better than I in the first round of the play-off and I was lucky to get another tie, at 75, aided by holing a short pitch at the fourteenth. In the second play-off I went pretty fast on the first nine and picked up four strokes. I thought I had won, sure. But Willie started back with a 2, got another deuce at the thirteenth, where I took a distressing 4, and caught me at the long fifteenth, where I made the mistake of forgetting my friend, Old Man Par, and went to playing Willie; I tried to get home with my second on an uphill hole of 555 yards, and break his back with a birdie 4, instead of which he got a par 5 and I a buzzard 6.

So Willie came back with a fine 33, playing sound and beautiful golf, and beat me by a stroke on the last green. We were just one stroke apart in 108 holes. But he was champion, and I was runner-up—again. . . . I've wasted some time wondering if I might qualify for the position of champion runner-up. I've been runner-up in seven open championships; three American nationals; one Canadian; two southern; and one Florida West Coast championship. All at medal play. That one little stroke a round certainly does make a difference in the records. The saving of one stroke per round would have won all these but the Canadian, when Douglas Edgar was a matter of sixteen strokes ahead of everybody. And there's always at least one stroke in every round you can figure (afterward) that you really ought to have saved. But I suppose it's all in the book, and if you had saved that stroke, you'd have dropped another.

There are always a number of strokes in a round that you might have dropped, too. But you don't think so much about them.

CHAPTER ELEVEN

THE BIGGEST YEAR

GOLF is a very queer game. I started the year 1926 with one glorious licking and closed it with another. And it was the biggest golf-year I'll ever have. Walter Hagen gave me the first drubbing, and of all the workmanlike washings-up I have experienced, this was far and away the most complete. He was national professional champion; I was national amateur champion; we liked to play against each other; and a match was arranged for the late winter season in Florida; a 72-hole affair, the first half at the Whitfield Estates Country Club at Sarasota, where I was spending the winter, and the second half a week later at Walter's course at Pasadena. Walter was simply too good for me. My irons were rather seriously out of line, it is true, but no excuses are to be offered when the other fellow, on two really great courses—I regard the Whitfield Estates course as one of the best in America—is never over par on any round, and is four strokes better than par at the finish on the sixty-first green, where the match ended with me sinking a forty-five foot putt for a birdie 3 in the effort to go a little farther, and Walter sinking a forty-footer for a half, to chop my head off. Walter played the most invincible match golf in those two days I have ever seen, let alone confronted. And I may add that I can get along very comfortably if I never confront any more like it. He beat me 12-11.

That match did me a lot of good, I think. I had been playing very good golf all winter, and in a series of seven fourball matches, with Tommy Armour as a partner, against pairs of the best professionals in the country, Tommy and I had not lost a match. I fancied I was in for a good season, and then this drubbing came along and showed up glaringly the defect in my iron play which had started troubling me at Skokie, in the open championship of 1922. I set to work on that department, and I think it was Jimmy Donaldson, who was with Armour at Sarasota, who gave me the correct line—too much right hand in the stroke. I worked on the irons whenever I had a chance up to the British invasion. And the irons served me fairly well the rest of the year. . . . Whenever I could get the feel that I was pulling the club down and through the stroke with the left arm—indeed, as if I were hitting the shot with the left hand—it seemed impossible to get much off the line. Curious thing. The older school of professionals always insisted the golf stroke was a left-hand stroke, you know.

The United States Golf Association named Watts Gunn and me on the international team of eight members to play at

St. Andrews, Scotland, for the Walker Cup; an event played every two years, alternately in this country and Great Britain. We also were to play as individuals in the British amateur championship at Muirfield, Scotland; and four of us—Watts, Roland MacKenzie, George Von Elm and I—were to stay over and play in the British open championship at St. Anne's-on-the-Sea, England.

And here's another odd quirk of fate, if it may be dignified by that name. I was getting awfully homesick—leaving my wife and little daughter (a year old), and the rest of my family; and I really wanted to get back a few weeks in advance of the United States open championship; and when I started in the British amateur championship May 24 I already had booked my passage home on the Aquitania, with the members of the team who were sailing two days after the Walker Cup match, which followed close after the British amateur. I had decided not to play in the British open, which was only a couple of weeks before our own open championship at the Scioto Country Club, Columbus.

I went fairly well in the opening rounds of the British amateur—they start the entire field playing 18-hole matches in that event, you know, and keep on day after day, two matches a day, until only two are left, who play a 36-hole match in the finals. I don't like 18-hole matches. I may be all wrong, but I can't like them. Too much can happen in one round, over which neither golfer has any jurisdiction. But no matter—they are coming into fashion in this country, too; and the last national amateur at Baltusrol, where they played two 18-hole matches to start with, saw the two ultimate finalists, George Von Elm and myself, almost knocked off in Round 1, George had to go to the nineteenth hole with Ellsworth Augustus, and I to the eighteenth with Dicky Jones.

Anyway, I got to the top of my game by the fifth round and shot my head off against Robert Harris, 1925 British amateur champion. I won nine of the twelve holes the match lasted, defeating him 8-6. And next morning a youngster named Andrew Jamieson, about my age, gave me a tidy lacing, 4-3, in fifteen holes on which he never was above par, and was twice below it, granting that the first hole is a par 5, on the measurement. I wasn't shooting par golf, but I wasn't so bad, at that. He just beat me.

Now, that was the sixth round, and everybody that morning was openly expecting me to breeze on through to the finals (the eighth round in British championships) and there meet Jess Sweetser, who, after a severe match with Francis Ouimet, another of our team, was going steadily along and seemed certain to win through the upper bracket.

I felt pretty blue when Jamieson stopped me. And more than ever I wanted to go home. But here's the working of fate. If I'd been fortunate enough to go on through and win the British amateur, I'd certainly have sailed for home a week later, on the Aquitania.

Then I got to thinking that if I went home now it would look somewhat as if I were sulking over failing to win the British amateur championship—the Lord knows I was disappointed, because I'd love to win it. But truly I wasn't sore. And I didn't want people to think so. Moreover, I remembered that I hadn't behaved very well on my first visit, five years earlier. And I thought I'd like to stay over and show people I really could shoot some golf, at times. I hadn't showed any golf yet, except that twelve-hole burst against Robert Harris. And so I thought I'd stay on for the British open, and try my best to show them a little good golf. I had little enough hope of winning the British open. No amateur had won it since 1897, when Harold Hilton's name went on the beautiful old trophy, five years before I was born. But I thought maybe I could make a decent showing, and anyway I was determined, no matter where I finished, that I'd not pick up this time. . . . The British are a wonderful sporting people, and I wanted them to think kindly of me and to believe I could shoot a little golf.

Jess Sweetser, a hero if ever there was one—he collapsed, dangerously ill, within ten hours after helping to win the Walker Cup, and he must have been ill in the championship—went on through several tough matches to the finals with A. F. Simpson and won handily, and we all headed for St. Andrews, the home of golf, where the international team matches were to be played the following Wednesday and Thursday.

We won the big cup again, by a single point, and I feel it was George Von Elm's grim battle with Major Hezlet, resulting in a halved match, that gave us the margin. Watts Gunn performed nobly, getting a lot of revenge on the Hon. W. G. Brownlow, a most engaging youngster who had put Watts out of the recent championship. Watts beat him 9-8 in the singles matches at St. Andrews, and Watts and I beat Cyril Tolley and Andrew Jamieson in the foursomes. I met Tolley in the singles division and had the first really satisfactory round I had yet played in Britain, which, with Tolley's wildness in the opening holes, put me 9 up in the first round and closed the match, 12-11, early in the afternoon. I was a stroke under par for the match and that is something to be happy about, on the Old Course at St. Andrews—to my way of thinking the greatest golf course in the world.

I was playing better than at any time since we had landed,

and went back to London rather glad I was to compete in the open championship. Freddie McLeod and I went over to St. Anne's for a few days' practice on the course, before the qualifying rounds, which I was to play with the southern section, at Sunningdale, in Surrey. I played only moderately well at St. Anne's, but as soon as I got to Sunningdale, I began perking up. . . . It's a wonderful course, Sunningdale, and I wish I could carry it about with me. I wanted to bring it back home, after the qualifying rounds. I shot a couple of practice rounds in 66—par figured strictly on our American yardage rating is 72. Anyway, I was going pretty well and had the feel of my iron shots as never before. . . . I said in the previous chapter it was as if I were playing the shot with my left hand and arm. And Sunningdale is a course with iron second shots. In my 36 holes there, in the qualifying round, I used a mashie twice and a mashie-niblick once, for approach shots. The others were good bangs with the irons, or a spoon, or occasionally a brassie. It's that kind of a course. The card shows it to be 6472 yards long, but it was a lot longer than that, from the tees we were using.

Well, when we started the first of the two qualifying rounds the course record was 70, and Archie Compston set a new record with a fine 69, early in the day. I was paired with a professional named Jones, oddly enough, and we had a big gallery.

I never hope to shoot a better round of golf than that one, in competition or out of it. The British critics said it was the finest round of golf ever shot in Britain; but they're very polite, over there. The score was pretty good; a 66. But it wasn't the score that pleased me so much as the way I managed to compile it.

This is the card:

Par (out). . . .	554	344	434 — 36		
Me.	444	334	434 — 33		
Par (in).	544	353	444 — 36	——	72
Me.	434	343	444 — 33	——	66

I was out in 33, and home in 33. I had 33 putts and 33 other shots. I had not a 5 and not a 2 in the card. And on only one hole of the round was I off the green with the shot which should have been on—the 175-yard thirteenth, when I shoved my iron slightly to a bunker and chipped out for a par 3. At the fifth hole I got down the only long putt of the round, a 25-footer, for a birdie 3. At the third, I missed a putt of five feet for a birdie; at the seventh I had a very simple looking putt of ten feet for a birdie and missed that. At the ninth, 270 yards, I drove over the green, chipped five feet from the cup—and missed the putt for a birdie. The score might have been better, you see. But I'm satisfied with it. The papers were awfully good to me. Mr. Bernard Darwin, I remember, characterized my performance in those two rounds as "incredible and indecent"—a wonderful line. . . . Lord, I was happy, after that round; and the one next day, when I got a 68 to go with it, and led the field by seven strokes! You see, I felt I'd showed them a bit of golf. And that was why I had stayed over.

Happy, and worried. I had sense enough to know I had come to the top of my best game six days before the championship, which was where I would need it. . . . Golf's a queer game. It comes and goes, and you cannot hold it. Anyway, I can't.

I won the British open championship, to quote Mr. Darwin again, without ever being quite on my game. Or maybe that *is* my game, and the scores below 70 are merely flashes. Anyway, my cards were 72-72-73-74—291. They look pretty regular, and they total as low a score as ever had been made in the British open championship, to that time. But I had to fight every hole of the way, to get them. There was never an easy round for me, over that sunny, wind-swept course at St. Anne's.

Take that first neat-looking 72. I was out in 37, missing the ninth green completely on a pitch downwind, and in order to come home in 35 I used only a single putt on the last four greens—two of 6 feet; one of 10; and the last one of 20. And I should be the last man in the world, I hope, to contend that that is golf.

The ninth hole had me. Pitching down the inevitable wind, using a spade or a mashie-niblick on a hole of 160 yards, I was on the green only one time in the four rounds, and then I took three putts. I never could hit the thirteenth green with my second shot, either; and as for that eleventh hole, 600 yards always against the wind—well, it was a new experience for me to bang three wood shots as hard as I could and then have a pitch left for the green.

I scraped my scores at St. Anne's if ever I scraped them; I used all the golf I knew, and right up to the last few holes it looked as if it weren't enough.

Walter Hagen led off with a 68 and fell away in the second round, and Bill Mehlhorn, another American professional, and I were tied for the lead. Two days gone—and Al Watrous, still another American pro, and I were paired for the third and fourth rounds; and I was two strokes better than Al at the start, and he did a grand 69 to my 73 in the third round, and when we went up to my room at the Majestic hotel for luncheon together, Al was leading the pack by two strokes, and I was second. Hagen was starting late that morning, and I told Al we'd better get away from the course and relax a bit; it's about the worst thing you can do, standing around the board waiting for some close rival to come in. So we went to the hotel and took off our shoes and lay down and had a bit of luncheon. It was a killing thing on both of us, being the leaders and playing together. But it's the break of the game. And I remember telling Al, as we started back to the club for the last round, to remember that the champion and the runner-up were in our pair. He's a great boy, Al Watrous.

On our heels were Hagen and George Von Elm, as we started the last round. It was something of a nightmare, for me. I hope I'll never have another such. My putting was ghastly—39 putts on 18 greens; never a green with only one putt; three of them with three. I hit the ball harder and harder off the tee, and I got farther and farther ahead of Al, in range. But it seemed I could never get those two strokes back. I couldn't help playing against Al. He was the opponent I could see and he was leading me. No matter what Hagen and Vol Elm might be doing, if I couldn't catch Al, they didn't matter. And it seemed I could not catch him. I blew a stroke at the inevitable ninth; I took three putts at the long eleventh—two chances gone. I missed the thirteenth green again, for the last time, with my iron. And I was two strokes down and five holes to play.

Old Man Par finished that round in the sweeping breeze. I managed to finish 4-3-4-4-4. That is just par. As luck would have it, it was good enough. At the seventeenth tee Al and I were level. His drive was straight and in the fairway. Mine was at the left, the ball on an imposing acreage of sand, with dunes between it and the green. Al played the odd and his ball was on the green. I had a medium iron left for a green I could not see from where I stood. I'll describe that shot more explicitly in a subsequent chapter. Anyway, it came off. My ball was inside Al's. He took three putts. I had a stroke in hand. I picked up another on Al at the finishing hole where his ball rolled into a bunker from the tee, and mine barely skirted it—plain luck. The two strokes were the margin. George Von Elm and Walter Hagen were tied, two strokes back of Al.

To me, John Henry Taylor, 56-year-old English professional, was the hero of St. Anne's. John Henry shot a 71 in a hard wind in the third round, in his gallant effort to stave off the rush of the American invaders. It was better than I could do in any round. And when I am 56 years old! . . . . My hat is off, to John Henry!

So I started home with the famous old cup, that has been in play since 1872, thirty years before I was born. Lord—I was happy! I felt when I saw the old Aquitania at Southampton, I'd pick it up in my arms and hug it! A wonderful voyage. And at New York, when the home folks from Atlanta came out on the Macom, to take me off at Quarantine, with Mary and Mother and Dad and Grandmother and Grandfather, and a lot of the boys. . . . and the band playing "Valencia". . . . You know, we marched up Broadway to the City Hall. . . . I can't talk about that, of course. But I'll never hear "Valencia" without my throat getting tight.

I went on to Columbus, for the United States open championship. Mary and Mother and Dad went with me. I was pretty well shot up and stale; it was only a couple of weeks after the British open. I had no idea of winning, and I was tremendously lucky to win, and I think it is a clear demonstration of destiny in golf that I did win. I'm glad I did, because I'll never have another chance to win both the British and American open championships in the same year, which hadn't been done before. But it was a miracle—a plain miracle, which must have been in the books before the tournament started.

I got away with a good first round and went all to smash in the second and was six strokes back of the field after finishing with a ghastly 7 on the last hole, two strokes being chucked away by childish, petulant mistakes. The morning of the final day I was sufficiently sick to go past a doctor's office and get something that was supposed to settle my stomach. The long strain had got me, I suppose. In some way I got through another good round, but was still three strokes back of the lead, then held by Joe Turnesa, who was playing about fifteen minutes ahead of me as we started the final round.

Stroke for stroke and hole for hole, we went the first eight holes of that last round. If Joe slipped, I slipped. If Joe picked off a birdie, I picked off a birdie. Until the short ninth, which was my *bête noire* of the tournament; a pitch from the tee on which I never was on the green. I missed it again; took a 4; and was four strokes down with nine holes to play.

Stroke for stroke we went on the next two holes—a par 4 at the tenth and another at the eleventh. This was not gaining anything, and the holes were running out. . . . I got a whale of a drive and a long brassie at the twelfth, a par 5 hole; got a short pitch fairly on, and holed a good putt for a birdie 4. My gallery let out a tremendous roar. Then I heard that Joe had taken a 6 on that hole, just ahead of me. Then I got back another stroke, and another—and one more, at the seventeenth. Joe rallied and shot a fine birdie 4 at the 480-yard finishing hole. I had a stroke in hand, and I hit that last drive with all I had. Judged by the second shot, I must have hit it 300 yards. I played a mashie-iron to the green; a running shot to a humped green, twenty feet past the hole. My first putt just stayed out. I was down in 4, a stroke ahead of Joe Turnesa. That was the championship.

But if anybody had told me, as I stood on the seventh tee, that I must finish with two 3's and ten 4's to win, I'd have laughed at him—if I'd had the strength. . . . Two under 4's, in that wind, and the last dozen holes of an open championship! Don't tell me it isn't destiny. Do you think I fancy for an instant I could ever do it again?

Well, I dragged myself back to the hotel with a lot of good players still out, not knowing who might catch or pass me, and (to tell the truth) so bewildered I didn't care much. I got to the room and Mother was packing my things and I blew up completely for the first time in my life. Anyway, I never did sit down and cry before. Mother said that would be about all of championship golf, for me. Next thing I knew they were calling me on the telephone, telling me to come out and get the cup. When we got back to Atlanta with the two cups—well, the bunch was all there!

So there was the Biggest Year I'll ever have, and all that remained was to round it out with another chastening in the way of a very fine licking by George Von Elm, in the final match of the 1926 national amateur championship at Baltusrol. I went there hoping to make it three national amateurs in a row, which hadn't been done—and hasn't been done yet. I was playing good golf, and won the medal in the qualification round. I got past Dicky Jones in the 18-hole first round, after a hard battle; and I managed to square off with Chick Evans in Round 3 for the drubbing he gave me at Memphis in the western, six years before—and a terrific job it was, too. Francis Ouimet and I met in the semi-final round and we had another fine battle, which I managed to win. I remember we halved ten consecutive holes in the morning round, and in the afternoon round we both were hot; I shot a 33 at him the first nine and picked up only one hole.

Then I met George Von Elm for the third time in three amateur championships, and George was too much for me. I played as well as I could, and played very good golf; I was a single stroke over par for the 35 holes the match lasted; and I had the breaks on a couple of stymies. George did not have the luck. He simply outplayed me. It was coming to him. I had beaten him at Merion and at Oakmont, and the Lord knows nobody is going to keep on beating a golfer like George Von Elm. I wanted to make it three championships in a row, but it wasn't in the book. It was George's turn. So the Biggest Year ended, as it began, with a beating.

Still, I'll always feel kindly toward 1926.

DOWN THE FAIRWAY

PART TWO

CHAPTER TWELVE

PUTTING: A GAME WITHIN A GAME

I WILL essay a few modest chapters in conclusion on my struggles with golf, and the playing of golf, with the emphatic understanding that there is nothing didactic about them. I am not attempting to give any sort of instruction, or to tell anybody how to play golf. Indeed, I am not at all sure I can make an acceptable job of telling how I play golf, myself. There are times when I feel I know less about what I am doing than anybody else in the world. But I *have* struggled with the game, and maybe I have learned a little as to how I play it. I have thought about golfing methods a lot; more than was good for me, I fancy. Stewart Maiden, the foundation of my game and my first and only model, says so, and I am willing to take Stewart's pronouncements concerning golf at face value. Perhaps some reflections on the method of playing certain shots will not be uninteresting; as I said, I've thought about these things a lot. But please understand I'm not commending these methods to anyone. I'm just trying honestly to describe the way I play certain shots. If anybody elects to try out these methods, it will be at his own peril.

Putting, a curious sort of game within a game, naturally comes first to mind. There is no need to labor its importance in golf. Nearly half the shots played by any expert performer are on the putting surface. Sometimes more than half. I recall with a mournful distinctness my last round in the 1926 British open championship when I used, or misused, 39 shots on the putting surface, and employed only 35 other shots.

At the start, putting was not a "game within a game," to me. It was nothing more than going up to the ball and knocking it into the cup, or making a free attempt to do so. I started playing golf with a sawed-off cleek. That was my outfit. And after I acquired some other clubs, I continued to use the cleek for putting, and as well as I can remember I did well with it. My first putter was an aluminum affair, a Ray-Mills model, and I seem to have done well with that, too, though I had picked up an interlocking grip somewhere which I soon changed to the Vardon grip used by Stewart Maiden. At the time, stance and grip and presence or absence of body-motion or knee action were as far from bothering me as Mr. Einstein's excursions into the realm of a supposititious Fourth Dimension.

But it seems I acquired a preference in putters, if not in the style of putting, for along in the winter between 1915 and 1916 I gave over the Ray-Mills putter for a Travis model; the small, wooden, center-shafted type with a brass face.

The first time I used it, I was playing with Mother at East

Lake, and the course was shortened by winter greens, and I shot a 66. I immediately concluded it was a good putter and became fond of it. That summer I won the Georgia state championship at Brookhaven, and, at the age of 14, went to Merion for my début in the national amateur championship.

The keen, fast greens baffled me there and I putted badly; I never had seen anything like those greens; in my first practice round I actually putted off of one green into a brook. Mr. Travis was there and took an interest in me and after I was beaten in the third round by Robert Gardner, Mr. Travis, the greatest putter the game has known, invited me to come out early next morning and said he would give me a lesson. We were traveling back and forth from Philadelphia by train and I missed a train and was half an hour late, and Mr. Travis declined to give me the lesson. However, he relented some eight years later, at Augusta, Ga., and gave me a lecture on putting which proved extremely helpful.

I needed help. From a fairly good kid putter, I became a wretched adolescent putter, having discovered how many things could happen to the ball in the course of three or four feet. That was always my hardest distance. It is today. There was a time when I honestly would rather confront a ten-foot putt that had to be holed than one of three feet. I felt I could at least hit the longer one.

I was a bad putter, or at best an indifferent one, up to Skokie, where the national open championship of 1922 was played and my putting held up a rather shabby game so that I finished in a tie for second place, a stroke behind Gene Sarazen. I was changing my putting style continually in those days, sometimes two or three times in the same round, so I can't tell you what was the matter; indeed, I think now it was not any one style or several styles at fault. I think I was thinking too much about how I looked—I was always trying to copy some good putter—and how I took the club back, and which hand I struck with, and a number of things other than the one thing to concentrate on—putting the ball in the hole.

At Skokie for the most part I was using a modified Hagen stance and trying to stroke the ball as he does. The Hagen stance has been often described—weight on the left foot; feet wide apart; hands well forward—you may see his hands apparently touching the crease in his left trouser leg. And Hagen, except for the holing-out putts of ten feet and under, when he takes the club back a very little way and strokes crisply and firmly with almost no swing, has a very perceptible motion or play in his knees, body and arms.

Now, I know that the accepted theory of putting is that the body and legs are immovable. But I think that theory is mistaken. Do not understand me as putting forward my own case; I am not a particularly good example. But take Hagen, Johnny Farrell and Francis Ouimet, three of the best putters I've ever seen. They take the club well back with a peculiarly free backswing; Farrell especially takes the club so high on the backswing for an approach putt that it would be a physical impossibility to get it there without a distinct "give" in the knees and body. And Francis moves his shoulders in the putting stroke. Can you move your shoulders without moving your body? I think not.

I know in my own case that some of my very worst putting is done when I am standing a shade too close to the ball, thus automatically cramping my legs and body into a certain rigidity. To my way of thinking there is no great peril in taking the club too far back in a putt, so long as the stroke is easy and free and rhythmical. Too much of a back-swing merely means easing the stroke a shade, while too short and rigid a back-swing, made with immobile legs and body, means, for me, a stabbed putt or one incorrectly hit.

There are other methods than the smooth swing, certainly. Years ago, Freddie McLeod was the deadliest putter at six and eight feet I have ever seen. He putted with such boldness that he fairly straightened out the line to the cup, hitting the back—and not only the back but the middle of the back—solidly and thus fairly ramming the ball home.

Being young and imitative, I naturally was fascinated by this daring style and tried it out. It would not work, for me. I was unable to acquire Freddie's superb accuracy; for the "door" to the cup when you are ramming them down is only an inch wide; you must hit that inch, or the ball probably will switch out. And I couldn't hit the middle regularly enough. So I worked around and imitated some other fine putters, with indifferent results, and finally, after years of suffering and tournament wrecks—I took 40 putts in one round of the national open of 1921 at Columbia—I finally arrived at the conclusion which obtains as these lines are written: that the best system for me is to stroke the ball with as smooth a swing as I can manage, and try always to gauge an approach putt, or any putt except the short holing-out efforts, to reach the hole with a dying ball.

Stewart Maiden had more than once urged this plan.

"When the ball dies at the hole," said Stewart, "there are four doors; the ball can go in at the front, or the back, or at either side, wherever it touches the rim. But a ball that comes up to the hole with speed on it must hit the front door fairly in the middle; there are no side doors, and no Sunday entrance, for the putt that arrives under speed."

This is especially true of keen greens. On a slow green you make take more liberties with hard hitting. But on the fast greens on which most championships are played—well, there's always that specter of the three-putt green. I had three of them, that last round at St. Anne's, in the British open championship of 1926. You don't forget those things, I can tell you.

Now, here's the way I look at it.

Too frequently, it seems to me, the famous old maxim of "Never up, never in," is made the excuse for banging the ball hard at the hole; and the player, seeing it run past three or four or half a dozen feet, consoles himself with the idea that at least he gave it a chance. And yet it isn't so much of a chance. Of course we never know but that the ball which is on line and stops short would have holed out. But we *do* know the ball that ran past *did* not hole out. That's another way of looking at it. And a putt that is struck too hard has only one way into the cup—through the middle of the front door, and then the backstop must be functioning.

Also, there is the matter of the second putt, not one precisely to be despised.

There is nothing—I speak from experience—in a round of either match or medal competition that bears down with quite the pressure of having continually to hole out putts of three and four feet; the kind left by overly enthusiastic approaches. For my part, I have holed more long putts when trying to reach the cup with a dying ball than by "gobbling" or hitting hard. And if the dying ball touches the rim, it usually drops. And if it doesn't touch the rim—well, you can usually cover the hole and the ball with a hat, which makes your next putt simple and keeps down the strain.

That is one thing that made the national amateur championship of 1924 at Merion so comparatively without tension. I was stroking the ball well and while I did not get down many long putts, my second putt usually was made from within a foot of the cup. It was there that Jerry Travers complimented my putting stroke, and I remember that I was using plenty of back-swing and rhythm; and I assuredly was not keeping my legs and body rigid.

Two putts stand out in my memory as illustrative of the value of getting the ball just to the hole. One sank. The other did not.

The first one was that forty-foot putt at Skokie on the fourteenth green of the final round, which gave me a birdie 3 and left me a chance to tie for the championship, which I later chucked away.

Now, heaven knows I wanted to sink that putt. Indeed, I *had* to sink one pretty soon or I'd never catch up. But I had stroked this one easily and the ball was trickling trickling toward the hole, and I was putting body-English on it with all my might, trying to pull it in, and I thought Joe Horgan, Duncan's caddy, was *never* going to pull that pin out. Just as the ball was six inches from the hole, the hypnotized Joe came to life and yanked out the pin. The ball rolled up to the hole, looked in, and dropped. So did I, on the green. I surely was pulling hard!

The other putt is even more clear in my memory; the putt on the thirty-fifth green at Memphis in 1920, when Chick Evans beat me 1 up in the semi-final round of the Western amateur championship, in the most exciting match I have ever played.

Chick had somewhat unexpectedly—to me, at any rate—got out of a grass bunker and holed a twelve-foot putt for a 4 and I was left with a putt of six or seven feet for the half. Now, I hit that hole almost squarely. But I had hit the ball a little too hard, and it slid around the rim and came out, almost on the same side as myself. There went the match and the championship, so far as I was concerned. I had attended most of all to getting the line. I got the line. But not the range.

I wouldn't say the range is more important than the line all the time, of course. In a holing-out putt of two, three, four or six feet, the line is almost everything and you don't have to worry much about the pace, if you get the ball as far as the hole and still don't bang it. But in the approach putts, I do think the range is the thing. Perhaps if I attended more to the line and not so much to the range, I'd get down in one putt more frequently. Also, I probably would take three more often. So it breaks no worse than even, I suppose.

I remember, too, my final putt at the Engineers Club in 1920, when an amateur team representing the United States met a team representing Canada, and I was playing Frank Thompson, and came to the final green with a twenty-five foot putt to square the match.

The ball stopped within a foot of the cup—short. I was beaten. As I walked off the green Johnny Anderson said to me, jokingly:

"That was a fine, bold putt, Bobby!"

I grinned and said yes. But down in my heart I knew I wasn't trying to get that ball *past* the hole, so if it didn't sink nobody would kid me about it. I was trying to get that ball *in* the hole. It's no trick, and not especially a symptom of courage, the way I see it, to bang a ball hard enough to make sure it's going past the hole if it doesn't happen to drop.

Now, I haven't said much about grip or stance because I've changed mine a good many times and may change them again, and anyway, I do not think the secret of putting, if there is a secret, is in the mechanics, granted that the swing can be made smoothly and to a fair degree automatically. I do say that for me there must be some flexibility, and hence movement, of the knees and body, and of the arms, in putts of some length. I keep my hands opposed; that is, with the palms opposite and the wrists thus working exactly against each other, which is not done in the bigger shots, where my left hand is more on top of the shaft and my right also a bit farther over.

But as I see it, the thing that hurt my putting most when it was bad—and it was very bad, at times—was thinking too much about how I was making the stroke, and not enough about getting the ball into the hole. I have always been a fair approach putter, and I am not so bad at holing-out now, though not in the class with a number I could name. But I have concluded that, having acquired a fairly smooth and accurate stroke, the thing for me to do is to forget it as far as possible and concentrate on getting the ball into the cup.

Which seems to have been the original object, in golf.

CHAPTER THIRTEEN

THE PITCH SHOT: A MYSTERY

IT seems to me that the more loft there is on a club, the harder it is to play. Why, I don't know. For years I have been wishing I could play a mashie-niblick shot the same as a mashie shot. But I can't do it. I'm not so bad with a mashie. But it seems the mashie, for me, is one of the irons and not one of the pitching clubs. Now, the No. 4 iron, which is just over a mashie in strength, and the mashie-iron are my favorite clubs. I will have some kind words to say of them when we get to the iron chapter. I can say right here that I'd far rather be left with a shot to the green needing a No. 4 or a mashie-iron—say 160 to 180 yards—than a shot needing a mashie-niblick, of from 100 to 120 yards. I'm more likely to be near the pin from the longer range. That is why I perform better, as a rule, on a long course. The drive-and-pitch courses which offer those alluring scoring opportunities to golfers like Walter Hagen, a veritable wizard with the pitch, are anything but friends of mine. Take the best round I ever played in important competition, the first qualifying round at Sunningdale, England, in the British open championship of 1926. There was next to no pitching to be done at Sunningdale. It wasn't a back-breaking course for length, but the holes were so arranged that, with acceptable driving, you needed either iron shots or wood shots or tiny pitches or chip shots to the green. I remember I used my mashie only three times there in thirty-six holes.

A sort of club-sketch of this celebrated course may not be out of order here; I liked it so much I wished I could carry it around with me; it suited my game so delightfully.

The holes are given with their length, the American par, the clubs I used, and the score of my best round in competition.

No. 1, 492 yards, par 5. A drive and a brassie. Two putts. Score, 4.

No. 2, 454 yards, par 5. A drive and No. 1 iron. Two putts. Score, 4.

No. 3, 292 yards, par 4. What is called a mongrel length. Drive and wee pitch to five feet from the pin. Missed the putt for a 3. Score, 4. This was not the type of pitch I dread.

No. 4, 152 yards, par 3. A mashie, 25 feet from the pin. Two putts. Score, 3.

No. 5, 417 yards, par 4. Drive and No. 4 iron to 25 feet from the pin. One putt (the only long one of the round). Score, 3.

No. 6, 418 yards, par 4. Drive and No. 4 iron to 18 feet from the pin. Two putts. Score, 4.

No. 7, 434 yards, par 4. Drive and No. 4 iron over hill to 10 feet from the pin. Missed putt. Score, 4.

No. 8, 165 yards, par 3. The others were using a mashie here. I used the No. 4 iron and an easy swing, shooting for the center of a dangerously guarded green, 40 feet from the pin. Two putts. Score, 3.

No. 9, 270 yards, par 4. Another mongrel, very interesting. A drive that rolled over the back of the small green. A chip to five feet from the pin. Missed the putt. Score, 4.

This put me out in 33 with 17 putts and 16 other shots and not a pitch except the wee one at No. 3. It was three strokes under par, based on the yardage.

No. 10, 469 yards, par 5. A drive from a hillside tee to a valley and a stiff iron shot to an upland green. My shot with a No. 2 iron was 30 feet from the pin and I was down in two putts. Score, 4.

No. 11, 296 yards, par 4. Apparently too short for a good hole, but very interesting; a blind drive with much grief if off line. I chipped to seven feet from the pin and got the putt down for a birdie 3.

No. 12, 443 yards, par 4. A drive and iron to 30 feet from the pin and two putts. Score, 4.

No. 13, 175 yards, par 3. A No. 4 iron and my first mistake

of the round; I think the only one. I shoved the shot out a bit to a bunker at the right, chipped six feet from the pin and holed the putt. Score, 3.

No. 14, 503 yards, par 5. A drive and brassie to the left edge of the green, pin-high. Two putts. Score, 4.

No. 15, 229 yards, par 3. A driving-mashie 12 feet past the pin, well in line. Missed the putt. Score, 3.

No. 16, 426 yards, par 4. A drive and iron to 40 feet from the pin. Two putts. Score, 4.

No. 17, 422 yards, par 4. A slight dog-leg to the right. A drive into the angle and the short rough and a No. 4 iron 30 feet from the pin. Two putts. Score, 4.

No. 18, 415 yards, par 4. A drive and mashie 30 feet from the pin. Two putts. Score, 4.

This gave me a score of 33-33—66 against a par of 36-36—72, with 33 putts and 33 other shots, only three of them being pitches of any description, and not one of them a pitch of the type that has come to be something like a *bête noire* to me. The Sunningdale course is 6472 yards on the card as we played it that day, and the setting of the tee-markers made it a good deal longer at some of the holes than the figures given, which are taken from the card. The only round I have had approaching it in important competition was my second in the southern open championship at East Lake the following year, when I shot a 66, with two approximate mistakes in it. But the East Lake course is perhaps three strokes easier, and I had a 2 and a 5 in that round, where I had nothing but 4's and 3's in the Sunningdale 66. I love a round with only 4's and 3's in it. The implication of such a round is that you are shooting golf and not carrying horseshoes.

Now, this is a rather lengthy and complicated digression, but the Sunningdale course persistently stands out in my memory as the one on which I could shoot my own game to the best advantage—which, please understand, is not necessarily a lasting compliment to the Sunningdale course, and certainly not to my game, which then lacked, as it does now, a good, reliable pitch shot of from 100 to 120 yards.

There was one hole at St. Anne's, where the British open championship was played, which called for a mashie-niblick pitch in each of the four rounds, and I was on the green only once—and then improved my good fortune by taking three putts. This was No. 9, a hole of 161 yards, admirably guarded. The distance indicates a mashie, or, in my case at times, even a No. 4 iron. But there was always a stiff following wind, and I used either a mashie-niblick or its slightly stronger companion, a spade. That hole became a nightmare for me, and it nearly cost me the British open championship.

Then there was the eighth hole at St. Anne's, which needed a straight drive along the boundary line and an approach, after a good wallop from the tee, of from 100 to 120 yards to a green situated on top of a sort of mound. This was just the range for a good mashie-niblick pitch and all the other fellows were playing it. But I didn't dare. Every time I played that hole—and I was fortunate enough to get really good, long drives to excellent position—I took my mashie and played a pitch-and-run into the front slope of the mound, trusting that the ball would run up on the green. I had not an idea of trying for the pin. I was just trying to get on the green. And where the other boys were getting plenty of 3's at that hole, I never could do better than par; and it was a hole where one might reasonably be expected to pick up a stroke now and then, if driving well.

Well, there are some illustrations of the disadvantage of not having a good pitch shot, to go with that course at Sunningdale, of blessed memory, where I didn't need one.

But what is the matter? Candidly, I wish I knew. There was a time, when the punched-face clubs were lawful, when I felt I had a decent control of the pitch shot to the pin, and loved to spank the ball boldly and firmly right at the flag. Even now, from a clear lie, I don't fear the shot unduly, and can usually bring it off with fair success, though I am far from a brilliant performer with it. But let the ball be lying in heavy grass, even in the fairway, or especially in clover—and I'm as helpless as possible. I can get the ball up, all right, but it is out of control on reaching the prosaic earth again. And I have seen it, projected from such positions, scampering across the green like a rabbit and disappearing into trouble beyond so many times that a species of buck-ague strikes me whenever I stand up to that type of shot.

There, to my mind, is the real strength of Walter Hagen's game. I know you hear more about his putting and his fine work about the greens, and that department is thoroughly praiseworthy; I do not know a better man about the greens than Walter. But I do not know as good a man with the mashie-niblick pitch; and I think there is his real power.

You see, a putt that any man holes over fifteen feet is somewhat lucky. You can't get away from that, or say that any man can count on holing such putts. But Walter's mashie-niblick plants that ball again and again right up against the pin, or within the range of six or eight or ten feet at which he is particularly deadly with the putter. Walter makes the putting easier, with that amazingly accurate pitch. And oddly enough the putting seems to get most of the credit.

I've studied Walter's method with the mashie-niblick a good deal, and I wish I could acquire something like it. He employs a club with less loft than the conventional type of mashie-niblick, and his shot is notably less steep. His backswing, it seems to me, is well on the flat side, with plenty of turn to the body. He brings the club on the ball with a magnificently crisp smack. All the stroke seems to go into the ball. There is no finish, to speak of. The ball flies extraordinarily low and evidently possesses terrific backspin, because it pulls up short on touching the turf.

That is a marked disadvantage of the steep or towering pitch, added to the exaggerated influence of the wind. A tall pitch loses so much of its backspin that when it touches the turf it is likely to be out of control. Six or seven years ago Francis Ouimet was using a markedly low pitch, with great effect. His pitch is steeper now, and the ball seems less subject to control after landing on the green—which, of course, is where control should be in evidence, if anywhere.

For myself, I have for some years taken advantage of whatever option was afforded me in reaching the green with a pitching club. Since the old days, when I could bang the ball up toward the pin without anything special to worry me; when heavy lies and clover were taken care of by the punched surface of the club which caused it to take hold of the ball under all circumstances—since those days are gone I have been pitching wherever possible without relying upon the backspin that is so essential a feature of the pitch-and-stop shot. I aim for a spot well in front of the pin, and let the ball roll on up toward the hole, where there is room. I should not call my shot a pitch-and-run, which is a special type, and really not what I should term a pitch shot.

There are, to my way of thinking, two kinds of true pitch shots. One is the straight pitch with strong backspin, in which the ball is struck firmly with a descending club—"knocked down," as the saying is—and a lusty divot is taken from a position an inch in front of the ball; that is, the club begins to take the turf about an inch after the ball has gone. The other type is known as the cut shot, in which the club comes on the ball from outside the line of flight, hitting more under the ball than down on it, and, as it is termed, "cutting the legs from under it."

This latter shot gives the ball a marked fade or drift to the right in the air, and it usually, because of this drift, breaks to the right more or less abruptly on touching the turf. It is a perilous shot for me, and one I rarely play except when compelled by exigency to bring the ball to a prompt halt as it reaches the green. Then I use a niblick, when the range is not too great for that club. George Duncan appears to me to employ a deal of cut in his pitches, and of course J. H. Taylor has the reputation of a cut-shot artist with the mashie and other pitching clubs, but I confess that in watching John Henry I could not see that he uses any extraordinary amount of cut in such shots.

Speaking of the niblick, I would like to put in a word for this much-misunderstood club. Most players regard the niblick as purely a trouble club, for blasting shots out of the sand and for hacking the ball out of the deep rough and from other horrid places. But to me the niblick is far more than a mere excavator. It is a trusty and effective pitching club from the fairway, and when I am confronted with a pitch up to 90 or 100 yards which must stop short on landing, instead of trying the cut-shot with a mashie-niblick, I like to play a plain straightforward pitch with the niblick, not bothering about any cut—the added loft of the niblick's blade takes care of the stoppage automatically. It is a grand pitching club, within its rather limited range; for me, at any rate.

No—the mashie-niblick and its slightly stronger brother, the spade, constitute for me the most puzzling problem in golf shots. I am fairly reliable with the niblick and with the mashie, though I confess to playing the latter precisely as I play a No. 4 iron, so that, as suggested earlier, the mashie falls naturally into the iron instead of the pitching category, in my play. There seems to be something different in my attitude toward the mashie-niblick, and certainly there is something different in my swing with it.

As near as I can figure it out, the main trouble is an inability to use my body in making a stroke with the mashie-niblick, especially for something like its normal range of 120 yards. I seem to take the club backward and upward in a line too near the line of play—too straight, in a word—and to employ my arms in a sort of pseudo-scooping motion in the actual stroke, just like any duffer, instead of smashing the ball firmly and allowing the club's natural loft to take care of elevation and backspin. It's a disgraceful thing to admit, but I never seem able to trust this particular club to do to the ball just what it is designed to do when properly swung—to elevate the ball and apply backspin and thus control it. I seem always to be trying to help the club, which is a most pathetic fault in golf.

Possibly this is a habit of mind growing out of a protracted slump with the mashie-niblick. Curiously enough, with the spade I am somewhat better; I don't seem to fear it will not get the ball up, though its loft is less than that of a mashie-niblick.

Thus I play the shot more decisively and with better results.

Another fault with the mashie-niblick is a disposition to keep my wrists too straight at the top of the swing; they are not "broken" sufficiently. This is detrimental to timing and takes out of the stroke some of the rhythmic snap so essential to the control of the ball.

Another disastrous mashie-niblick hole here obtrudes itself—the seventh at Flossmoor, where the national amateur championship of 1923 was played, and where Max Marston beat me in the second round, this hole playing something of a figure in the sudden burst of birdies with which Max wiped out my slender lead and went out in front in the afternoon round. This hole is a typical mashie-niblick pitch across a little lake which stretches from the edge of the tee to the edge of the green; absolutely all carry. Max had just picked off a birdie 3 at the difficult sixth and had squared the match. Using that curious, full swing with a pitching club he had planted the ball about a yard from the pin on the little lake hole, and of course I had to get within reasonable putting range or another hole was gone. I missed the shot and the ball missed the green—on the front side. It splashed. Max got a 3 on the next hole and I never caught him.

With all its crimes, the mashie-niblick has served me a good turn or two, and I shall always like to recall the one at Scioto.

This was at the fifteenth hole of the final round in the United States open championship of 1926; the sixty-ninth of the competition, when I was one stroke back of Joe Turnesa, who was playing a couple of holes ahead of me. The hole is a dog-leg, bending to the right; a drive and pitch. I had cut the angle too close with the drive and was left with a pitch from the rough, which was sedge-grass at Scioto, about 120 yards from the green over a dangerous bunker, with a hard breeze off the left. This was my worst range and the wind complicated the stroke further. I had to pitch, and I had to get a 4 on that hole, Joe having just made one. Here I had a bit of luck. Somebody earlier in the day had played a shot from the very spot where my ball rested, shaving the tall sedge-grass so the ball had a clean lie, though nothing to boast about. I managed to get hold of the ball well, it was almost exactly on line, and well on the green though 20 feet short of the pin. I can tell you, I was relieved when I saw the finish of that shot!

Bobby finishes a three-quarter iron shot from a tee in the 1923 Open championship.

CHAPTER FOURTEEN

IRON PLAY: I LIKE IT

THERE are times when I am convinced that I actually know something about playing the irons—almost. Also, there was a time along in 1925 and 1926 when I was thoroughly convinced I neither knew anything about playing the irons, nor would ever know anything about it. I began to suspect that no one else knew anything about playing the irons, so far as helping me out was concerned.

I was discouraged.

Sad iron play at Worcester in 1925 had beat me out of the national open championship. There was no room to doubt that, because I can remember one round where I lost five strokes from iron shots not one of which was extremely terrible, but all of which were just enough off-color to land in a carefully placed bunker. If they had been worse shots they wouldn't have been so bad, you might say. As I came out in a tie with Willie Macfarlane after 72 holes, and lost to him on the thirty-sixth hole of the play-off, I think I am warranted in accusing those iron shots of my downfall.

Then I did pretty well at Oakmont with the irons and won the national amateur championship, and the following winter I spent most of the time at Sarasota, Florida, and played more golf than I had ever played before in the off-season, and felt I was set for a big year when Walter Hagen came along and gave me the sincerest lacing I've ever received, in a 72-hole match.

Now, I'm not going to charge the irons with that cataclysm. Walter was shooting such fine golf that I am certain he would have beaten me anyway. He was in a simply tremendous mood, and when he is in the humor—well, I have plenty of distinguished company among the victims of Walter's rampages. But the irons were sour again and cost me a good many of the holes which finally exterminated me, 12-11, so far from what might have been the finish.

I repeat, I was discouraged. And the British tour was in prospect.

As to what was wrong, it was pretty much everything. I was not even consistent in ill-doing. One iron shot would be swung around to the left; another would be shoved out to the right. It got to be a standing joke, around the Whitfield Estates golf course, the way I could miss the green from 180 yards with the shot that counted, in a friendly round with Jimmy Donaldson and Tommy Armour, and then in a rage throw another ball down on the turf and bang it up against the pin.

Jimmy used to ask me why I didn't play the second ball first, and insist that I was getting my right hand too much into the stroke, and I got to thinking almost exclusively about my left hand and began getting some control of the ball, though, hit in that manner—as if the left alone were doing the job—it invariably went with a fade which had to be allowed for.

I didn't care for this type of shot, though I've been told that Harry Vardon in his palmiest days played virtually every iron to the green with a trace of fade and gained great control thereby.

The idiosyncrasy must have been perceptible, at least to the expert critics, because the first thing Mr. Harold Hilton commented upon, after watching me in a round at St. Andrews, was my manner of playing the iron shots.

"Only a genius could manage it," said Mr. Hilton. And he told me I was coming on the ball from outside the line, on every shot, and that but for superior timing and touch I would be ruined a dozen times in the round.

But I couldn't change then, in the thick of the British campaign, though I hadn't done so well at the British amateur championship at Muirfield. There were three great events, you see. The British amateur, which Jess Sweetser won, I being put out in the sixth round by Andrew Jamieson; the Walker Cup, or International Match, at St. Andrews, and finally the British open championship at Lytham and St. Anne's. And I couldn't go monkeying with my swing radically. I talked with George Duncan about it, and played a number of rounds with him, and George is far and away the greatest theorist in golf. But I got through the Walker match pretty well, and shot two good rounds at Sunningdale, qualifying for the British open—mainly by not forcing my iron play in the least. I tried always to take a club a shade stronger than was needed, and to hit the ball cleanly and easily. I hate to keep referring to that round of 66 at Sunningdale, but a very great deal of it was iron play; almost no pitching at all. And I managed very well by not forcing the shots.

Still, there was a shot in each round; an iron shot, that I had to lean against. It was the drive on No. 15, a sweet one-shotter of 229 yards over level terrain; which means the yards all were 36 inches. It was a fairly narrow shot to that green, too, and a big iron was indicated, if you could sock it, and would.

I suppose I was pretty well keyed up in both those rounds, and the hole just looked like my old driving-mashie to me, the strongest iron I carry. And in some mysterious fashion I socked that ball right past the pin both rounds, nearly hitting it, the ball being twelve feet past the hole the first round and fifteen feet past it the second. I remember those iron shots very pleasantly, and Mr. Bernard Darwin was kind enough to compliment my second shot on No. 10 in the first round, where I got hold of another one, with a No. 2 iron, and hit a shot of about 200 yards up a steep hill over a big bunker on to the green and got a birdie 4.

And of course it was an iron shot won me the British open championship.

Curious thing, now I come to think of it. In the winning of three national open championships, one British and two United States, there has invariably been one single iron shot that did the trick. You see, the boys never let me get away with anything like a lead. When I managed to win the British open with a two-stroke margin, I felt I had spread-eagled the field; the result was never in doubt after the 72nd hole! I had to play off with Bobby Cruickshank to win the United States open of 1923, and I had to play the last dozen holes at Scioto in 1926 in ten 4's and two 3's to nose out Joe Turnesa by a single stroke.

And in every case an iron shot stood out most obtrusively.

The one against Cruickshank at Inwood is mentioned rather fully in a preceding chapter. It was with a No. 2 iron. The following year I sent that iron to a dear friend, the late

Mr. J. S. Worthington, who was going home to England—to die, as it turned out. He wrote me not long before he sailed and asked me for one of my discarded clubs, as a sort of keepsake. There was only one that I thought enough of to send him; the one that got me my first big championship.

This shot at St. Anne's, and the one at Scioto, were each with a mashie-iron, but not with the same one, as I gave the first one to Charlie MacFarlane right after the tournament. Charlie was very kind in what he said about that shot. It was at what might be called a crucial juncture.

The seventeenth at St. Anne's is a hole of 411 yards, with apparently acres of sand along the left side of the fairway, all done out in dunes. The hole bends to the left and the sand is not a good place to play your second from. Added to the native disadvantages of a sand lie, from the position in which I found my ball after a slightly pulled drive I could not see the green at all. Al Watrous, with whom I was paired, had lost a lead of two strokes and we were level with two holes to play. Here he had a good drive and his second was on the green. As suggested, it was a critical position.

The only way I could get a good look at the green, and what lay between it and my ball, was to walk far out to the right, nearly across the fairway. I did this. The prospect was not precisely encouraging. I had to hit a shot with a carry of close to 175 yards, and hit it on a good line, and stop the ball very promptly when it reached the green—if it reached the green. This, off dry sand, though the ball luckily lay clean, was a stiff assignment. You know, an eighth of an inch too deep with your blade, off dry sand, and the shot expires right in front of your eyes. And if your blade is a thought too high—I will dismiss this harrowing reflection.

Anyway, I played the shot and it came off, and the ball

stopped closer to the pin than Al's and he took three putts. This gave me a stroke in hand which was tremendously needed, and I had some luck at the last hole on both my drive and my second shot to get a par 4, Al losing another stroke by visiting a bunker which I missed by a couple of feet, at least.

The same type of club—do you wonder I'm fond of the mashie-iron?—came out for the final shot to the green at Scioto fifteen days later, on the last hole of the United States open championship. As I stood on the last tee I was told that Joe Turnesa had finished with a birdie 4 on a hole of 480 yards. I had a stroke in hand and a birdie would keep me in front of Joe; and there was better than a fair chance that I would win the championship, as the closest competitors were not going any too well.

I hit that drive as hard as I could. There was a cross wind off the right but it did not seem to affect the shot. When I got to the ball, near the left edge of the fairway, I needed a poke with the old reliable mashie-iron, a bit more than a half swing, to get home. It was about 180 yards, but I did not want to play a shot that carried to the green, which was slightly domed; what is called a turtle-back. It was a dangerous business, banging the ball firmly to that type of green, and I decided on another kind of shot. I hit a rather low ball, aimed to carry to ten or fifteen yards in front of the green, it being perfectly open, and run the rest of the way. The line was good and the range near enough right; the ball ran about 20 feet past the pin. I had two putts to finish in front. The first one was very close. I won the championship by one stroke.

I love the irons. And knocking about a good deal I have gradually accumulated a set which seems to fit. They've been copied by Tom Stewart at St. Andrews and by Victor East, of the Spalding company. Mr. East, a designer and golf club engineer, told me the micrometric measurements and the scientific weighings and testings showed that in my own crude and purely instinctive way I had assembled, all unknown to myself, a perfectly coordinated set of clubs. All but the mashie-niblick, said Mr. East. It was a sort of maverick. I have felt for some years that there was something wrong with that darned club!

My set is not at all a regular series. Like my wood clubs, they tend less to loft than the models generally accepted as standard. I carry, in the descending order of power, a driving-mashie, a No. 1 iron, a No. 2 iron, a mashie-iron, and a No. 4 iron. As suggested in a previous chapter, the mashie, which comes next, also seems like one of the iron series to me. I do not carry a No. 3 iron. The mashie-iron, which I like better, takes its place.

Club nomenclature has changed much in recent years, and I may explain that the old driving-iron now is classed as a No. 1. The driving-mashie, a somewhat stronger club, is deeper and shorter in the face, and is a shade heavier. The No. 2 is what used to be called a midiron, but mine is straighter in the face than the usual No. 2 and is nearly like a No. 1 out of stock. My mashie-iron is nearly as straight as the old-fashioned midiron. My No. 4 perhaps is nearest the conventional model, being only a shade straighter. The widest gap in my series is between the mashie-iron and the No. 4.

It is next to impossible to assign a range of shots to these clubs, because the choice of a club depends less on range than on the character of the shot, and all shots are subject to almost infinite variation, due to terrain, wind, and other circumstances. If there is such a thing as a normal range under normal conditions, I should say that for me the No. 4 is good for about 160 to 175 yards; the mashie-iron up to 190 yards; the

No. 2 something like 200 yards; and 210 to 220 yards for the No. 1 and the driving-mashie, though you may be sure that if my spoon is in working order I rarely call on the irons for a shot of that length unless the lie or other circumstances indicate an iron.

Yes—I love the irons, even if sloppy play on the second hole at Skokie was costly in the national open of 1922, and looseness at Worcester ruined me in 1925. I've studied the irons a lot, and listened to many a lecture. The last one I listened to was the shortest, and it seems to have done the trick—for the time being, at any rate.

Genius or no genius—remembering the delicate compliment of Mr. Harold Hilton—I got away fairly well in Britain with an iron play that was never really satisfactory except at Sunningdale, which was a matter so exceptional that now I feel I must have been hypnotized. At Sunningdale, with its profusion of iron shots, I had the feel of the clubs to an extent that made it seem utterly out of the question to be off line.

But I wasn't satisfied with the somewhat compromised style in which I was hitting the irons, and when I got home to Atlanta after the big journey of 1926 I went out and had a little talk with Stewart Maiden, who to me will always be the first Doctor of Golf. I suppose I did a little confessing.

Stewart said:

"Let's see you hit a few."

I hit a few. Stewart seemed to be watching my right side. He is a man of few words.

"Square yourself around a bit," said he.

I had been playing a long time with a slightly open stance, my right foot and shoulder nearer the line of the shot than the left side.

"Move that right foot and shoulder back a bit," said Stewart.

I did so, taking what is called a square stance.

"Now what do I do ?" I asked Stewart.

"Knock hell out of it!" said he, concisely.

I did. The ball went like a ruled line.

That is Stewart Maiden's method of teaching or coaching. In this imperfect and complicated world I have encountered nothing else as simple and direct. Stewart saw that my swing was bringing the club on the ball from outside the line of play. He didn't bother with explanations or theories—he never does. He settled on one single thing by way of adjustment. It worked. That is a prime feature of his adjustments.

In a general way this is my method with the irons.

I try to hit the shot straight; that is, without fade or drift to the right or draw to the left, except when a cross wind indicates the desirability of what is known as "holding up" the ball. Even in that case the result is a line shot, if it is properly executed.

My stance for the irons is approximately square; that is, with my feet equidistant from the line of play—not from the ball, which is opposite the left foot. My left arm is straight, not theoretically but actually, from the moment the turning motion away from the ball is well started until sometime after impact. I try always to turn well away from the ball in the back-swing. In this motion I am conscious that the left side is pushing the right side away from the ball. At the risk of becoming tiresome let me repeat that this free body-turn seems to me the most important factor of my swing.

With no wind to consider, I try to play a straight and simple shot, using a club a little more than adequate to get the distance, rather than taking a full crack with a club just strong enough. I rarely knock the ball down with an iron or play that used to be called the push shot; very popular with many fine players formerly.

With the wind off the right or against, I like to take a club appreciably stronger than the range warrants. It is a curious fact that a slower hit causes the ball to bore better into a head-wind, perhaps by reason of carrying less backspin. And when the wind is off the right, the tendency being to impart a bit of cut to a shot with a stronger club, the ball is held up, in a manner of speaking, into the wind and proceeds in a straight line.

With the wind off the left, I like a weaker club than the shot indicates and a harder smash in the stroke. I play the ball a bit farther from me and hit it hard, with a slightly freer turn of the body. My right shoulder, too, comes in a little higher, inducing a slight draw; that is, a faint curve to the left, which holds the ball up into the wind. It should be remembered, however, that unless the wind is very strong it has little effect, right or left, on a properly struck iron shot; and these refinements are not often essential. Of course the wind will increase or curtail the range of a shot, and that is taken care of by the selection of clubs. As stated, I like a stronger club and a slower stroke against the wind, with a lower trajectory and relatively more wind-jamming power. You are shooting against a fine cushion, so you don't need to worry about stopping the ball.

With a following wind I like a weaker club, swung harder. This adds elevation to the stroke, which is needed, as a following wind seems to take spin off the ball or at any rate minimize its controlling effect on landing.

I am aware that these minor variations are likely to appear as affectation, and I trust the reader to believe that my game never was built up and developed with any such things in mind. I suppose they came along subjectively, instinctively; and I know that most of them are performed with perfect unconsciousness in playing the round, just as an outfielder in baseball cuts loose for the plate with no thought of the position of his feet or the juncture at which his wrist snaps, or anything beyond sending the ball on a proper hop to the catcher. It is impossible to describe most of these little refinements of the golfing stroke. You just do them, when your subjective experience tells you to, mostly without any objective thought. It is a fascinating sort of thing to try to analyze, and I hope earnestly that my analytical efforts will not result disastrously for some confiding reader.

CHAPTER FIFTEEN

THE HEAVY ARTILLERY

I AM not going to attempt separate consideration of tee shots and wood shots through the green. In the essential points I think they are sufficiently similar to permit a discussion of the drive to answer for all.

A reduced brassie of Mother's was the first wood club I possessed and often I played all the way around the course with no other clubs, when Mother and Dad would let me tag along with them on condition that I would keep up. I never did much on these excursions except keep up, as you may imagine. In my earliest outfits I used wood clubs with rather shallow faces, and the best driver I had as a kid was one with a big yellow head which Alex Smith had made for Perry Adair before I started golf; Perry had outgrown it. Stewart Maiden made my first regular set of clubs; a driver, brassie, midiron, mashie, niblick and putter. I knew nothing of the spoon or the baffy in those days, which may account in some degree for my wood clubs being less lofted today than those regarded as standard models. The conventional wood clubs, according to Victor East, a great designer, are lofted in the following degrees: Driver, 79 degrees; brassie, 75; spoon 71. My own set is considerably straighter in the face: Driver, 82; brassie, 79; spoon, 73. This makes my brassie of the same loft as the conventional driver. This is supposed to be the straightest-faced set in use today.

The vast range of the modern golf ball has reduced the use of brassie and spoon play among the experts; but the brassie and spoon shots are comfortable things to have working for you; when you need one, you usually need it very much indeed.

When I was a kid I loved to slug, and got away with it fairly well with the irons, but with the wood I was frequently off line, usually on the left. This must have been due to overly enthusiastic hitting, because, as recalled earlier in this book, there was a tournament at Knoxville, when I was 14, when I drove accurately in every round because I had lumbago and couldn't try to kill the ball.

When we suggest that slugging is the cause of a certain error in play it may be as well to go a bit farther, for hard hitting has, I think, been held too generally responsible for too many golfing idiosyncrasies.

My main fault as a youngster, and the one I have to guard against now most carefully, was stopping the left side before impact; failing to let go, I should call it. Whatever was the reason for *that* failure in the old days, before I knew what caution was, it would seem that an excess of care is responsible now, as

I usually commit this particular crime at a most inopportune juncture, as when confronted with a narrow fairway. When I let go and hit hard the ball usually goes pretty straight.

A good example of this fault may be taken from the 1927 southern open championship at my home course, East Lake, in which I drove consistently well except that I never could hit a good ball from the first tee. Some 250 yards from the tee the fairway narrows between a clump of trees on the right and the lake on the left. I ought to be accustomed to that situation after all these years, but in this tournament I seemed unable to let myself go into the shot, and in every round discharged a wretched shot, the last two being such especially terrifying efforts that I was lucky to have my ball stay out of the lake.

For the drive with the wood, and for all normal wood shots, I play the ball opposite the arch of my left foot. This is pretty well forward, and a great many very fine players have the ball farther back. Along in 1923 and 1924 I also was playing the ball farther back, which was a departure from Stewart Maiden's method, and was not done with any conscious design on my part; I think now I just got careless as to the position of the ball and perhaps did not realize as I do now how important it was for me to keep the ball well forward. Some players like to hit the ball a descending blow with the wood clubs; but it seems to agree better with my method to hit it as fairly as possible in the back.

Anyway, during this period of negligence in placing the ball, I went in for clubs deeper and deeper in the face. You see, with the ball straying back between my feet, inches behind the line of the left heel, I naturally was hitting it a descending blow and the tendency was toward a climbing trajectory with more height than I wanted and little run at the

The "Dixie Whiz Kid" with a trusted wood, circa 1921.

Bobby practices for the 1922 Southern Amateur Championship at East Lake Golf Club.

end. I felt I was losing length and that the type of shot I was hitting was handled too freely by the wind, if any. So I tried out club after club, deeper and straighter in the face—a series of unhappy experiments which culminated in the winter of 1923-4 when I was at Harvard with the design of a driver which I fancied would be just the thing for me. I worked a long time at this design and when made up for me it was indeed an odd-looking club.

The head was not of the so-called Dreadnaught type, which is long and wide and rather shallow, so the title promptly bestowed on my pet bludgeon, the Super-Dreadnaught, was entirely a misnomer. This head was little if any larger than the usual head, fore and aft. But there was a lot of wood in it just the same; as Virgil might have said, it was no small part of a tree.

The face was 1⅝ inches in depth, with a bulge of ⅜ inch, and virtually no loft at all. I suppose it was as near a 90-degree club as ever was used from the tee. There was so much wood in the head that a tiny pellet of lead was all the weight it would carry, and I seem to recall some of these heads made up without any lead in them at all.

When you have a fancy for a club you frequently do well with it, for a time, even if it is not truly suited to you. Being the daddy of this one I naturally was fond of it, and, while it was, in plain language, a stupid attempt to correct a faulty position with a freak club, I really did some very good work with it in the spring of 1924, and in the open championship of the Georgia-Alabama Professional Golfers Association, at the Druid Hills club, Atlanta. I took it to Detroit for the national open championship that year at Oakland Hills, but a persistent attack of smothering the ball caused me to change after a couple of rounds to a more conservative model, and soon after that I discovered that my trouble lay in the position of the ball, since when my clubs, though distinctly of the deep-faced type, are quite conventional models.

This freak design of mine caused a good deal of comment at the time, and a little discussion of my efforts with it may be of some interest here, especially as illustrating certain points which go to make up whatever I have of method in wood club play.

I had overdone the thing, in this design. I wanted a club that would keep the ball rather low in flight, without the disposition to climb which was bothering me, and give it a good run at the finish. I found I had to play the ball opposite my left foot, if I were going to get it up at all with this design. And I had to tee the ball nearly an inch high, so I could smack it fairly in the back. When all was going well and I was hitting accurately, I got some really notable results. I think I never drove better in my life, and certainly not as far, as in the Georgia-Alabama open event. I remember that at the eleventh hole Charlie Hall, the famous Birmingham slugger, with whom I was paired, got away a drive of 360 yards and I nearly matched it with one of 340 yards; the two pokes aggregated just 700 yards. And I got a longer one, potentially, at the fourteenth hole of the same round, where the drive goes straight against a sharply ascending hillside leading up to the green, 340 yards away. With no help whatever in roll, my shot there was just off the corner of the green. I think that is the longest ball I ever hit, for carry, though some have traveled a good deal farther before they stopped rolling.

But I had overdone the matter. The ball had to be struck with such scrupulous precision to get it up that the least variation resulted in a badly missed shot, usually smothered. I was getting the ball forward to what I later ascertained was its correct position, for me, but I needed a club with a greater margin for error.

Smothering the ball, I am happy to say, is pretty much a thing of the past with me. I get an occasional shot well off line to the left, from a locking of the left hip and the ensuing valiant effort of the arms to hit hard anyway, without free transit for the body; but usually these days when I am off line it is to the right.

There are two reasons for this: Carelessly getting the ball a couple of inches too far back at the address, and failing to get the club head through in time. In effect, the club head meets the ball somewhat before it has got to the proper place in its arc.

I have come to regard a free body-turn as the most important factor in my own method, and of course the legs and hips are intimately connected with body-turn. I wonder if I can describe it acceptably.

In addressing the ball preparatory to a shot with the wood, I must not be too far away; having to reach for the ball invariably spells trouble for me. I stand up fairly straight and my feet are close together, comparatively. The stance is about square; that is, with the toes nearly the same distance from the line of the shot. The left toe may be a shade farther from the line; ever so slightly an open stance, as it is called. In the address, my weight is on the balls of the feet, as near as I can perceive equally distributed between them.

Now as to weight transference.

It's a sort of queer thing to say, but to me it seems my weight is transferred to the right and then to the left, in the backward swing and the stroke, and *also* in a kind of four-cornered figure, back and forth, as well as sideways.

As stated, the weight at the address is distributed between

the balls of both feet, the knees being ever so slightly bent forward. Going back, the weight comes over to the inside of the front of the left foot, as the left heel rises and the left knee knuckles inward, the transferred weight settling very solidly on the right heel at the top of the swing. This transference is reversed in the stroke; the weight now coming over off the toe of the right foot, as the right heel rises, and settling solidly at the finish on the left heel.

This complicated-sounding process, as suggested, is vitally connected with body-turn; and I am prone to regard it as essential to me in all shots, big or little. Of course in the smaller shots the body-turn and transference of weight may be so tiny as hardly to be perceptible. But I think they are present and voting, none the less.

I play a straight left arm in all full shots from the time the club has started back until after the ball has gone. There is no easing of the elbow at the top of the swing. The straight left is encouraged by, and may be partly attributable to, body-work. George Duncan's idea is that the back-swing is started by a motion of the left side, body, arm and leg, beginning to turn. I think he is exactly right; also that this turning movement at once frees the left arm and makes it possible to keep the elbow straight and at the same time take the club upward and backward around the body without lifting it too much in the line of play; in a word, without having to take it back too straight.

In my own case, too, I am persuaded that the instinctive need for a free body-turn is responsible for the closeness of my feet together in all shots. The critics say my feet are closer together than anyone else's. But I never am conscious of any lack of balance, and if I attempt a wider stance, I simply cannot get a free enough body-turn.

If there is any special merit in my style of play, it is the free body-turn. Of this I am convinced.

Now, the hitting area in the down-stroke does not begin at the top of the swing, and the first motion of the club should not be inspired by the wrists; that is, the club-head should not start first, which would use up some valuable wrist action before hitting is possible. For me, as near as I can work it out, the correct way to start the down-stroke of any full shot is a slight sway to the left. The arms get under way with the wrists still "cocked," or wound up. It is a difficult sort of speculation, but it seems to me that the hitting area starts at that part of the stroke when the right hand begins to assert itself, the right arm begins to straighten out, and the wrists begin to unwind. In my stroke, this seems to be when the club is about parallel with the ground and the hands opposite the right leg. I suppose the speed of the club, from a gradual beginning, has been sharply accelerated to this juncture, and then the unwinding wrists and the straightening right arm provide the punch in the stroke.

It seems fearfully complicated, this trying to take a swing to pieces and see what makes it tick. I'd hate to try to learn to play golf synthetically. These attempts at analysis are quite puzzling enough. But it has been deeply interesting to me, in my feeble efforts at analysis, to encounter so many times, and in so many ways, the factor of body-turn in all shots.

One bit of earnest admonition. Stewart Maiden maintains that he cannot think of any of these details, or of any other details, during the execution of a shot—that is, if the shot is to come off. He adds that he does not believe anybody else can think of these or other details and perform a successful shot. I find this to be the case with my own play. I have to do all my thinking as I prepare to play. Once the swing is under way, the only thing I can think of is hitting the ball. To attempt to think of anything else is the most certain method of courting absolute ruin.

CHAPTER SIXTEEN

MISCELLANEOUS SHOTS—AND TROUBLE

AS a general proposition I fancy it might be laid down that the main object of a trouble shot in golf is to get out of trouble. This conclusion is not so obvious as at first it may appear, especially in the case of the average golfer, or worse. In that case, the object, or it might be better called the perilous ambition, is not only to get out of trouble but also to achieve a shot the equivalent of that which might have been made had the element of trouble not been injected.

He wants to get there, anyhow.

Now this ambition is in a way laudable, and at times it is grimly necessary to execute a shot which will minimize the punishment for getting into trouble. But it should always be borne in mind that, if a brilliant recovery be needed, it is far more feasible to make this brilliant effort *after* getting the ball back into a thoroughly playable position.

Now, I can speak with considerable feeling, if not with authority, on this point. The greatest improvement in my game in the last five years has been a growing disposition for calculating a difficult situation, and an increasing distaste for the taking of reckless chances. In the old days, furious with myself for the missed shot that had incurred the trouble, I was quite ready without further consideration to go up to the ball and put my back into a shot designed without delay to take up the slack. Now, I figure the chances a bit—sometimes.

Let us examine a troublous situation or two.

The ball may be in the deep rough, or in the woods, or in a side bunker, or with something intervening between it and the objective. What to do?

Of course there is a vast difference between match and medal play, and it is a favorite maxim of the match-players that one's policy on any one hole should be governed by the immediate situation, and by the state of the match. This is obvious, to an extent. There is no sense playing cautiously to halve a hole when holes must be won. And it is true that a ruinous score on one hole in a match means only one hole gone, while in a medal competition it may well mean the tournament; still, it doesn't damage your ultimate chances to devote some thought to the situation.

That is what I mean by figuring the chances. And the first question to be asked, considering a recovery shot, is: Is the shot practicable? Is the ball lying so that the chances are on your side in hitting it for the kind of shot you desire?

Further, *if* the shot fails to come off, will you be worse off than you would be by playing a careful, safety stroke out of the trouble?

There is where you may gamble a bit, you see. I try to figure it that way. And by way of illustration allow me to outline my own play on one hole in the 1926 United States open championship at Scioto, and on another, in the 1927 southern open championship, at my home course, East Lake in Atlanta.

The latter instance first.

Starting the third round of that competition, I pulled my drive to a peculiarly difficult situation behind some trees at the edge of the lake, which encroaches upon the left edge of the fairway some 240 yards from the tee. I found the ball lying well on the bank of the lake, with a decently large opening through the trees in the direction of the green. In an informal match some days previously I had driven to almost the same spot and had played through the trees to the green for my par 4. This was different. A championship was at stake in that tournament, at medal play. So I looked over the situation, concluded that I assuredly would *not* be as well off after a failure of the recovery shot—it almost certainly must have wound up in the lake, unless it came off—turned my back on the flag, and chipped modestly to a safe place in the fairway. From there I had a comfortable shot to the green, and a 5; not so good as a 4, certainly, but infinitely better for my state of mind, as well as for the card, than a 6 or a 7—or an 8.

The tenth hole of the first round at Scioto, in the national open championship of 1926, offered a somewhat different problem, though my drive there was certainly as terrible as the one at East Lake.

From the tenth tee at Scioto I shoved one far off down the hill into the sedge-grass rough at the right, with three trees between the ball and the green, which was guarded by a stream in front. One of those trees, the tallest, was directly in line. And the rough was *rough.*

Also, the distance to the green was about 175 yards, with that towering tree to carry.

All right. What was the option? To play back to the fairway was not easy. I could not chip safely out of that rough; I should have to hit the ball hard; and there was a good chance that I would find myself in the rough at the other side, or in some other situation not much of an improvement over that which I now occupied.

If I tried for the green, one of two adverse things might happen to the shot. I might hit the tall tree; or I might fail to get the ball away sharply enough and with sufficient smash to clear the tall rough. In either case, I should still be left with a decent shot at the green, which was all I could hope for, if I played back to the fairway.

I decided to go for the green, and I think I never hit a ball any harder. I used a mashie. The ball got up smartly, cleared the tree, reached the green on the carry, and pulled up at the farther edge.

I guessed right in that instance, and guessed safely in the other. Here is one in which I did neither.

This was in my younger and more impetuous days; in 1921, when the United States open championship was played at the Columbia course, Washington, D. C., and for the first and only time that most abominable notion, the 18-hole qualifying round, was employed, when one bad hole almost certainly meant a failure of qualification.

I began my qualifying round with a ghastly hook from the first tee, the ball disappearing into a thick wood at the left of the fairway, which inclined to the right on a typical dog-leg hole; a drive-and-pitch hole, par 4.

I found the ball lying on a bare spot, with a fair avenue through the trees toward the green, which could be reached by a medium iron shot. The only obstruction was a large log lying right across the line to the green, about a dozen feet from my ball.

As suggested, I was young and foolish, and the green was there in plain view—reasonably plain view—and I was in no mind to write off a stroke and chip carefully out to where I would have a perfectly clear pitch to the green; a certain 5; and a fair chance, by getting the pitch close, or holing a good putt, for a par 4. That, incidentally, is what I meant by suggesting the propriety of deferring one's brilliant effort until the ball was in a good position for it.

So I banged gallantly away at the ball, determined to place it on the green. But as I was coming on the ball I thought of that big log; I remember it distinctly. I flinched, half-topped the shot, and in the twinkling of an eyelash I was standing there listening to the rebounding ball hitting tree after tree *behind* me. Yes, and I heard one other thing. Some of the more fervent members of the gallery had followed me into the forest to see the shot played; and I heard one of those chaps who can't possibly whisper, but always rumble, say with an appalling distinctness:

"There goes Bobby!"

I didn't need that to complete my discomfiture. I knew there was one good chance that we'd never find my ball, and another that it would take several strokes to get it out of the woods, if we did find it, and that in either case—well, I wouldn't qualify for play in the national open championship of 1921. And failure to qualify—well, it's a tragedy, no less.

It was luck saved me. We did find the ball, and it was in a position where it could be played, though not with any ambition to get on the green or near it. I played out carefully, was on in 4 for a sorry 6—and ultimately qualified with a single stroke to spare. It was that close. See how much more comfortable a 5 would have been! After a missed pitch at the seventeenth, I holed a 30-foot putt, to save that single stroke for qualification.

So I can't help the opinion that it is judgment more than mechanical execution that counts, when you're in trouble.

The latter phase is not particularly complicated. Ordinarily, when in trouble, the ball is in heavy rough or in a bunker. In long grass, there is nothing much to be done except to select a club sufficiently lofted to get the ball up sharply, so that it is in the air before the grass smothers it. Unless the grass or rough is extraordinarily heavy it is better to attack the ball with the idea of hitting it accurately rather than slugging it. Brute force sometimes must be called on, but as a rule I try to hit the ball fairly in the back, with an ascending stroke and all the club under the ball at impact.

Bunker play from the sand, except around the green, is rather hard to describe. Near the green I seldom use a full blasting or explosion shot unless the ball is in a deep lie, such as a heel-print, or in one of the furrowed traps like those which are traditional at Oakmont, where the sand is raked every morning before the day's play into ridges between which the ball invariably settles.

To blast, I stand normally, lay the club off a bit—that is, lay back the face a trifle more than usual; the club of course being the niblick—and hit hard into the sand a distance behind the ball designed to regulate the length of the shot. This may be anywhere from just back of the ball to a couple of inches, depending on the texture of the sand and the range. The idea is to project the ball from the sand without the club's face touching it; the ball literally is exploded by the impact of the sand, and emerges flying dead, without spin, and usually subsides with little run, when the shot is made properly. There are occasions when only this shot will suffice.

When the ball is lying clean on the sand you have the option of the chip, which is played as if the ball lay on cement, and is dangerous, since you have two ways of missing it badly—either taking the ball too high in the back, with the effect of topping it, or of taking sufficient sand to kill the stroke.

My favorite shot from a clean lie on the sand near the green is neither a blast nor a clean chip. It is a half swing in which some sand is taken, but in which the club's face reaches the ball.

I take a normal stance, the ball opposite my left toe, and an upright position. I use the niblick, with a full shaft. I always take about the same length of stroke, a half swing, and govern the range by the amount of power applied. It is easier for me to control than the clean chip, but it must be understood that it is far more perilous than the frank blast, since there is little margin for error in the strength of the swing or the amount of sand encountered by the blade of the club. I certainly do not recommend this shot to the general run of golfers. It needs a lot of experience, and I know of no manner of describing it helpfully. You swing just so hard, and take just *so* much sand, and there you are—or there you *aren't*. I like the shot because I've been sort of raised on it. I do not know where I picked it up, but I've practised it a lot, even in hotel rooms. The sand factor in some way is comparable to the nap on a heavy carpet, and I've practised the shot by placing the ball a yard from a bed and trying to pitch the ball on to the bed and stop it there. At the Del Prado Hotel, Chicago, we used to have competitions in the room, and I remember executing one shot at the ninth green of the Flossmoor course, in a practice round before the national amateur championship of 1923, which seemed to please a considerable gallery.

The ball lay in a plain pot bunker with square sides, some two feet below the surface of the green, the hole being cut very near that side. I played the old bedshot, and the ball went spinning up by the pin, twisted about as if a magnet were holding it, and stopped two inches from the hole. Except where strokes are vital, I'd much rather lay a ball dead from a bunker than hole it. In the latter case the gallery concludes it's luck. So do you. In the former case—great shot!

It was this type of shot with which I extracted the ball from the right-hand bunker on the fifth hole at St. Anne's, in the 1926 British open championship, and got it close for a par 3 after a somewhat wandering tee-shot.

Among the miscellaneous shots the chip stands out with such prominence as a stroke economist that I feel it should be considered as one of the distinctive strokes in golf, and one of the very most useful.

Par allows us two putts to the green; 36 in the round. But who is it plants the proper shot on the green steadily, for even one round? So far as memory serves, I never have seen it done. Somewhere I have heard that championship golf, round after round, averages 32 putts. This means that on at least four greens the player has got down in a single putt. And in most instances, that putt resulted from an accurate chip, taking up the slack of a bigger shot which just failed of its aim.

The chip is the great economist of golf. And in the period when I was looser with my irons even than at present I had perforce to cultivate a decent chip shot, or lose altogether too many strokes. I have no need to explain that I need it frequently today.

I employ no particular club for the chip, but try to play the same kind of shot with several clubs—ranging from the mashie-iron straight down to, and including, the niblick. This gives a variety of loft, naturally, and rather than alter the stroke to govern the proportion of chip and roll, I simply select the club.

Many good players prefer one club for the chip, and adjust the carry and the roll by the stroke, turning the blade over at impact to provide less carry and more roll, or sending the blade straight through and wide open, to apply "drag," with a longer pitch and a shorter roll.

I like to play every chip with the nearest edge of the putting surface as a target. If the green is close and the pin well back from the edge, I use a mashie-iron, the loft of which will just drop the ball on the smooth putting surface, running it the rest of the way. If the ball is farther from the green, or the pin nearer that edge, I take a more lofted club, always trying to hit the same way, a straightforward stroke with no turn-over and no cut. Let me repeat, the edge of the putting surface as a mark at which to chip is a great help.

There is another kind of shot from just off the putting surface to which I am partial, when the intervening turf is fair and true; a sort of extended putt, with a little old cleek the original of which was designed by John Morris of Hoylake, long before I was born. The shaft is rather soft and of putter length; and the stroke is only a big putt, and I have found it pretty reliable in getting the ball at least decently near the hole.

Those little shots from just off the green—they're the least spectacular in golf, I suppose, and the greatest stroke-savers, if they are working for you.

CHAPTER SEVENTEEN

TOURNAMENT GOLF

EARLY in this little book I made the statement that there were two kinds of golf—golf, and tournament golf; and that they were not at all the same. In this concluding chapter I shall try to go a little into the difference, with special reference to tournament golf, because, whether justly or unjustly, a golfer in these days is judged principally upon his tournament record and his tournament achievements.

I think a man may be a truly great golfer and not be a great tournament golfer; and I do not think that the customary implication, that a great golfer who fails to shine at formal competition lacks courage, is justified. Matters of physique and mere physical stamina have a profound effect, as do also personal inclination and taste. Then there is that curious and little understood factor of temperament, which is so convenient an explanation either of the successful tournamenteer or the unsuccessful one.

In any event, I maintain that golf and tournament golf are two different things; and it may be that I can speak with a little show of authority from acutely personal experience, since for a number of years I was regarded as a great golfer, and most certainly as not a great tournament golfer. I had a remarkably good opportunity to study the difference, which was increasingly heavy upon me in those years while I was competing in eleven major championships, and never winning one. A great golfer—but he can't win championships. That was what they said; kindly, but with a sort of conviction.

Now, I did not lack confidence, in my earliest championship tournaments. I was very young and brainless; I didn't know enough to fear the competition or to worry about it. And even then tournament golf was different. Especially the big tournaments. There was something about it; something that seemed to key me up, not unpleasurably. I began to notice that I seemed to play better when nervous. This is true today. The most unpropitious symptom I can experience before an important round, of match or medal play, is absence of nervousness. It is a rare thing for me to be able to manage even the restricted tournament breakfast, the morning on which the big show starts.

Digressing a moment, I might explain here that I play better fasting. That is one of the changes since I grew up. As a boy I loved to eat; I still love to eat, but not on the days of tournament play, until after the second round. I used to eat plenty of breakfast of my accustomed kind; oatmeal, bacon and eggs, all too frequently cakes or waffles; and coffee. And at luncheon between rounds, hungry from the exercise, I would not think of denying myself something substantial, topped off by a pie *à la mode*. Pie and ice cream—with an afternoon round to play!

Not any more. For breakfast, when I can eat, a strip of bacon and a small chop and a cup of black coffee. For luncheon, between rounds, a slice of dry toast and a cup of tea.

There is another difference between just golf and tournament golf. Playing an exhibition match, I eat—and drink—whatever I please between rounds, and seem to play none the worse for it. In fact, I could tell you the story of a match Max Marston and I played against two professionals, where our host took us to his home for luncheon between rounds—we were all square at the end of the morning round and having a hard battle—and administered to my unsophisticated palate five or six pleasant-tasting cocktails, whose bland guise concealed a mighty kick. When I reached the club for the afternoon round, I had to get very carefully out of the motor car, and while teeing my ball I was concerned with my balance. This state of affairs, of course, should have been ruinous. But such are the vagaries of golf, when the tournament strain is not on, that instead of disgracing myself hopelessly in the matinee round, I led off with a 3 at each of the first three holes, finished with a 66, and our side won the match, 6-5.

Not in tournament golf. I have a good, big dinner in the evening in my room, prefaced by two good, stiff highballs, the first taken in a tub of hot water; the finest relaxing combination I know; and then a few cigarettes and a bit of conversation, and bed at 9 o'clock. And usually I sleep well, despite the curious strain that is always present, in championship competition.

Some of the best informal rounds I have played followed closely on the heels of dietetic eccentricities that would cause the coach of a football team to faint in his tracks. But, according to our little maxim, there is golf—and tournament golf. And in the latter I try to take no more chances than I have to. There are chances enough, at the best.

It must be a sort of subjective nerve-tension, this difference in tournament golf. Years ago I discovered that the best preparation for a big tournament, for me, was as much rest as I could acquire, in the twenty-four hours before the opening gun. In my younger days I liked to play a lot of golf, right up to the day the competition began. Often I'd play 36 holes the day before it started. Now I try always to schedule the little preliminary practice season, of three or four days, so that the last day I can rest. In bed, often, with a book. I remember the day before the national amateur championship at Flossmoor, I stopped in bed and read Papini's "Life of Christ," a book with an odd fascination to me. If I can avoid it, I never touch a golf club the day before a big competition opens, and I prefer to play only 18 holes a day the two days preceding.

The fair success of this plan induces the opinion, then, that the strain of championship golf is mostly mental; and certainly the mere physical strain would not burn one up as has been my experience in so many tournaments. Could anyone make me believe that six days of just golf, 36 holes a day, would have stripped eighteen pounds off me, as that six days at Oakmont, in 1919, did? At Worcester, in the open championship and play-off of 1925, I lost twelve pounds in three days, and I wasn't much overweight when I went there. Perhaps these physical symptoms help to explain the furious toll exacted from the spirit, under the stress of tournament competition. I know that tournament golf takes a lot out of me; the photographs, before and after, sometimes are rather shocking in contrast.

Now, my career to this writing, which includes the year

1926, is divided with so extraordinary a balance as regards tournament golf and championships that it would seem there must be a good opportunity to offer something in the way of a solution of the difference between a good golfer and a good tournament golfer. In the seven years between 1916 and 1922, inclusive, I played in eleven national championships, and did not win one. In the four years including 1923 and 1926, I played in ten national championships, winning five and finishing second three times.

Something, then, seems to have happened, to fatten the run of what one fanciful writer termed my seven lean years. And here it seems I have worked up to a climax, without the climax—excepting a negative sort.

There has been a change in my tournament attitude; of that I am sure. It was not an improvement in shot-making. Leaving off the minor refinements, I had as good an assortment of shots in the seven lean years as I have today. I think I never played particularly badly in any of those tournaments, before I broke through to win. I know that in the amateur competitions I never was beaten by a man who was not playing first-rank golf. And as I began to read more and more, and hear more and more, the dictum that I was a great golfer, but I could not win a major championship, the sorry option seemed forced upon me that either I was jinxed—a wretched sort of plea—or that I didn't have the tournament stuff. . . . I pondered that miserable option more than I would care to have people know.

There must have been a change in my tournament attitude, then. But I cannot say surely when it came about, or how. Certainly I did not go to Inwood in 1923 for the national open with any fresh access of confidence. I think I never was less confident. I had been beaten until I was expecting it. Also, I was not well, and I was playing wretchedly.

Yet I won that championship, after tying with Bobby Cruickshank; and I think that perhaps it was in that tournament my attitude began changing. I saw Jock Hutchison leading after the first round and the second, collapsing midway of the third round. I saw Bobby Cruickshank, going to the fourteenth tee of the final round in a dazzling burst of golf—he went through seven holes, beginning with No. 6, in 23 strokes—break down even as I had broken down in my own finishing round, and tie me by shooting a wonderful birdie 3 at the seventy-second hole. And I managed to beat him in the play-off.

So I suppose I began to understand that the other fellows all had their troubles, too; that I didn't have to go out and shoot four perfect rounds to win a major open championship, or even one perfect round, if I could just keep four decent rounds sticking together. I suppose I began instinctively to understand that the tournament strain bears down on everybody; not only on me. I suppose I began to understand that one lost stroke did not necessarily have to be redeemed at once; perhaps it was not ruinous; perhaps the other fellows were losing a stroke, too.

Now, if this was a change in mental attitude, it was not complete by the time we played the national amateur championship at Flossmoor that year, and Max Marston put me out in the second round. But I do think the alteration crystallized between Inwood, 1923, and Merion, 1924. Perhaps at Flossmoor.

I got a severe lesson and a drubbing in the second round. I had played well enough in the qualifying rounds to tie with Chick Evans for the medal score, and as he also was retired early from match competition, we played off the tie the following day. At the fifth hole Chick, playing grandly, was leading me by two strokes—medal play.

Now, on the previous day when Max Marston had got me two down in the afternoon round, I remember thinking I must get those holes back right away—*right away*. And I never could get them back, hard as I tried.

In this play-off with Chick, at medal competition, I was two strokes down. But I had a different attitude. Some way, I wasn't in that frantic hurry, about getting those strokes back. It was as if something deep in my consciousness kept counseling patience. Patience! Somewhere lately I heard or read that the greatest asset of Harry Vardon was his perfect realization of the cold fact that no matter what happened, there was only one thing for him to do—keep on hitting the ball. I hadn't heard or read that, at Flossmoor; and I cannot say that such a plan was in my mind. Indeed, I had no plan. Instinctively or otherwise, I managed to keep on hitting the ball, and not trying to wrench back those strokes immediately. And presently—presently they came back to me, in a sort of normal and ordinary manner, and some more with them.

So maybe that is the answer—the stolid and negative and altogether unromantic attribute of patience. It is nothing new or original to say that golf is played one stroke at a time. But it took me many years to realize it. And it is easy to forget, now. And it won't do to forget, in tournament golf.

Mostly I've had to run behind, in the major championships. The only important medal competition in which I went into the last round with a comfortable lead was the southern open championship of 1927, at my home course, East Lake, and I hardly knew what to make of the situation—being eight strokes ahead of the field. But in the major championships I've managed to win, I've usually had to run behind. At Inwood I fancied I had a good lead in the closing round—and I did not run well in front. Maybe that taught me something; that when I was behind, I did not need to load myself with additional worries about the man who was setting the pace, because he probably had his own troubles. Anyway, I was running behind right up to the closing holes of the British open and the United States open of 1926, and if anything pulled me through it certainly was not courage, but just patience, and managing to keep on hitting the ball. At Scioto, in the United States open, indeed, I was so far behind there was no use going out to pick up strokes. As I stood on the seventh tee of that last terrible round, if someone had come to me and said: "You will have to do these last twelve holes in two under fours to win," I should have known surely that it could not be done. Yet that is precisely what *did* have to be done, to win. And by managing to play those twelve holes one hole at a time, and one shot at a time, I scraped through.

Maybe that is the answer—patience. Whatever I may possess of it now must have been cultivated, as I assuredly did not have it at first, and the number of years required to hammer it into me is a sorry commentary on my native intelligence.

It's a long way from that first round of 80 at East Lake, when I was a skinny kid, running to show my card, which I made Perry Adair sign, to Dad; my first real bout with Old Man Par, and, I suppose, the first glimmering notion that here was the real opponent.

After all, it's Old Man Par and you, match or medal. And Old Man Par is a patient soul, who never shoots a birdie and never incurs a buzzard. He's a patient soul, Old Man Par. And if you would travel the long route with him, you must be patient, too.

I really think that is good advice. I hope I may be able to follow it, occasionally.

Tournament golf! It's different from just golf in other ways, especially when it leads at last into the cage of championship. I read a line somewhere, or a title, "The Cage of Championship." It *is* something like that. Something like a cage. First you're expected to get into it, and then you're expected to stay there. But of course nobody can stay there. Out you go—and then you're trying your hardest to get back in again. Rather silly, isn't it, when golf—just golf—is so much fun?

Still, championship has its compensations. There was that sight of New York harbor, in 1926, when I was bringing the British open championship cup home; New York harbor, and the Macom coming out, with the home folks aboard, and the band playing "Valencia." . . .

I've been awfully lucky. Maybe I'll win another championship, some day. I love championship competition, after all—win or lose. Sometimes I get to thinking, with a curious little sinking away down deep, how I will feel when my tournament days are over, and I read in the papers that the boys are gathering for the national open, or the amateur. . . . Maybe at one of the courses I love so well, and where I fought in the old days. . . . It's going to be queer.

But there's always one thing to look forward to—the round with Dad and Chick and Brad; the Sunday morning round at old East Lake, with nothing to worry about, when championships are done.

DOWN THE FAIRWAY

CHRONOLOGY

CHRONOLOGY

The Major Events in the Golf Life of Bobby Jones

1911—Age 9

Won junior championship cup of Atlanta Athletic Club.

1912—Age 10

Lost to Howard Thorne in semi-final round of the same championship.

1913—Age 11

Shot his first 80, on the course at East Lake.

1915—Age 13

Lost in the finals of the second flight, Montgomery invitation.

Qualified 3rd in Southern amateur, lost second match to Commodore Heard, and lost in final of beaten-16 championship division, called second flight.

Won invitation at Roebuck Springs, Birmingham.

Won Davis and Freeman cup at East Lake.

Won East Lake club championship.

Won Druid Hills club championship.

1916—Age 14

Lost to Perry Adair in semi-finals, first flight, Montgomery invitation.

Won invitation, Country Club, Birmingham.

Won invitation, Cherokee Club, Knoxville.

Won invitation, East Lake.

Won Georgia state amateur championship at Brookhaven, Atlanta.

Lost to Robert A. Gardner in third round of national amateur at Merion, Philadelphia.

1917—Age 15

Lost to Louis Jacoby in second round of Druid Hills invitation.

Won Southern amateur championship, from Louis Jacoby, at Roebuck, Birmingham.

1918—Age 16

Red Cross matches.

War Relief matches at Baltusrol, Englewood, Siwanoy and Garden City. Won three singles and two foursomes; lost one foursome with Perry Adair to Emmett French and Jack Dowling.

1919—Age 17

Lost to Nelson Whitney in semi-finals of Southern amateur at New Orleans.

Runner-up Canadian open to Douglas Edgar—tied with Jim Barnes and Karl Keffer, 16 strokes behind Edgar.

Runner-up to Jim Barnes in Southern open.

Runner-up to S. Davidson Herron in national amateur.

Qualified in Western amateur. Lost in first round to Ned Sawyer.

First entered national open at Inverness, Toledo, finishing with 299, four strokes behind Ted Ray's 295, which won the tournament.

1920—Age 18

Tied with Willie Macfarlane for eighth place, national open, Toledo.

Won Southern amateur, Chattanooga.

Won medal, Western amateur, Memphis, and lost to Chick Evans in semi-finals.

Won medal, national amateur, Engineers' Club, and lost to Francis Ouimet in semi-finals.

Won medal and first flight, Morris County invitation,

Morristown, N. J.

Runner-up to J. Douglas Edgar in Southern open.

1921—Age 19

Lost to Allan Graham in fourth round, British amateur, Hoylake, England.

Won singles and foursome matches in team matches, America vs. Britain.

Withdrew 11th hole, third round, British open, St. Andrews.

Tied for fifth place in national open, Columbia, Washington, D. C.

Tied with Joe Kirkwood for fourth place in Western open, Oakwood, Cleveland.

Lost to Willie Hunter in third round, national amateur, at St. Louis.

1922—Age 20

Tied with John Black for second place, national open, Skokie.

Won Southern amateur, East Lake.

Finished in fourth place, Western open, Cleveland.

Won singles and foursome matches in Walker Cup matches, National Links, Southampton.

Lost to Jess Sweetser in semi-finals, national amateur, Brookline.

1923—Age 21

Won national open at Inwood after play-off with Bobby Cruickshank.

Won medal, national amateur, Flossmoor, Chicago, after play-off with Chick Evans. Lost to Max Marston in second round.

1924—Age 22

Runner-up to Cyril Walker in national open, Oakland Hills.

Won national amateur, Merion, Philadelphia.

Won singles, lost foursome, in Walker Cup matches, Garden City.

1925—Age 23

Lost to Willie Macfarlane in play-off of national open, Worcester, Mass.

Won national amateur, Oakmont.

1926—Age 24

Lost special match, 72 holes, in Florida to Walter Hagen, 12-11.

Second in West Coast open, Pasadena, won by Walter Hagen.

Lost to Andrew Jamieson in fifth round of British amateur, Muirfield, Scotland.

Won singles and foursomes in Walker Cup matches, St. Andrews.

Led southern section qualifying for British open at Sunningdale, England, 66-68-134.

Won British open, St. Anne's, with score of 291.

Won American open, Columbus, O.

Won medal, national amateur, and lost in final to George Von Elm.

1927—Age 25

Won Southern open, East Lake.

Finished in quadruple tie for eleventh place, national open, Oakmont, with 307 total.

GLOSSARY

For the 2001 Edition

Baffy: The equivalent of a modern-day approach wood.

Brassie: The equivalent of a 2-wood.

Cleek: A driving iron.

Dormie: In match play, being dormie means leading one's opponent by the same number as the number of holes that remain. The worst a player can do is finish the match in a tie.

Gutta-percha (Gutty): A substance made from the sap of certain Malaysian trees that was used to make golf balls, called "gutty balls," in the late 19th and early 20th centuries.

Mashie: The equivalent of a 5-iron.

Mashie-iron: The equivalent of a 4-iron.

Mashie-niblick: The equivalent of a 7-iron.

Midiron: The equivalent of a 2-iron.

Niblick: The equivalent of a 9-iron.

Spade: The equivalent of a 6-iron.

Spoon: Technically any high-lofted wood, but often used to refer specifically to a 3-wood.

Stymie: A term that refers to the pre-1951 rule that no player was allowed to pick up his ball once on the putting green. If another ball lay between a player's ball and the hole, that player was "stymied" and was obliged to putt over or around his opponent's ball.